done in a day

Calgary

→ The 10 Premier Road Rides!

Where to invest your limited biking time
to enjoy the greatest scenic reward

by KATHY + CRAIG COPELAND

hiking camping.com

Heading outdoors eventually leads you within.

The first people on earth were hikers and campers. So today, when we walk the earth and bed down on it, we're living in the most primitive, elemental way known to our species. We're returning to a way of life intrinsic to the human experience. We're shedding the burden of millennia of civilization. We're seeking catharsis. We're inviting enlightenment.

hikingcamping.com publishes unique guidebooks – literate, entertaining, opinionated – that ensure you make the most of your precious time outdoors. Our titles cover some of the world's most spectacular wild lands.

To further support the community of hikers, campers, and cyclists, we created www.hikingcamping.com. Go there to connect with others who share your zeal, to plan your next trip, or to stay inspired between trips. Get advice from people returning from your destination, or share tips from your recent adventure. And please send anything you want to post that will assist or amuse the rest of us.

To fully benefit from, and contribute to, the book you're now reading, visit www.hikingcamping.com and follow this path: Guidebooks > Cycling > Canadian Rockies > Done in a Day: Calgary > Field Reports.

nomads@hikingcamping.com   hiking camping.com

MEMBER
1%
FOR THE
PLANET

Businesses donating
1% of their sales to the
natural environment

www.onepercentfortheplanet.org

Copyright © 2007
by Craig and Kathy Copeland
First edition, December 2007

printed on
recycled paper

Published in Canada by
hikingcamping.com, inc.
P.O. Box 8563
Canmore, Alberta, T1W 2V3 Canada
nomads@hikingcamping.com

All photos by the authors

Maps and production by C.J. Chiarizia
giddyupgraphics@mac.com

Cover and interior design
by www.subplot.com

Printed in China by Asia Pacific Offset

Library and Archives Canada Cataloguing in Publication

Copeland, Kathy, 1959-
    Calgary : the 10 premier rides / by Kathy & Craig Copeland.
(Done in a day)
Includes index.   ISBN 978-0-9783427-3-9

    1. Cycling--Alberta--Calgary Region--Guidebooks. I. Copeland,
Craig, 1955- II. Title. III. Series: Copeland, Kathy, 1959- Done in a day

GV199.44.C22W58 2007   796.52209711'31   C2007-902715-6

Contents

TRIPS AT A GLANCE

The trips are listed according to difficulty, starting with the easiest and working up to the most challenging. After the trip name is the round-trip distance, followed by the elevation gain.

1	Lake Minnewanka	15.5 km (9.6 mi)	142 m (466 ft)
2	Waskasoo Park	30 km (18.6 mi)	80 m (262 ft)
3	Tour de Canmore	40 km (25 mi)	300 m (984 ft)
4	Elbow River Valley	60 km (37.3 mi)	500 m (1640 ft)
5	Drumheller	80 km (50 mi)	160 m (525 ft)
6	Sheep River Valley	76 km (47.2 mi)	645 m (2116 ft)
7	Highwood Pass	34 km (21 mi)	536 m (1758 ft)
	Highwood Junction	108 km (67 mi)	1267 m (4157 ft)
8	Bow Valley Parkway	99 km (61.5 mi)	360 m (1181 ft)
9	Waterton Lakes Park	66 km (41 mi)	595 m (1952 ft)
10	Icefields Parkway		
	Bow Summit	74 km (46 mi)	479 m (1571 ft)
	The Crossing	146 km (90.5 mi)	1103 m (3619 ft)

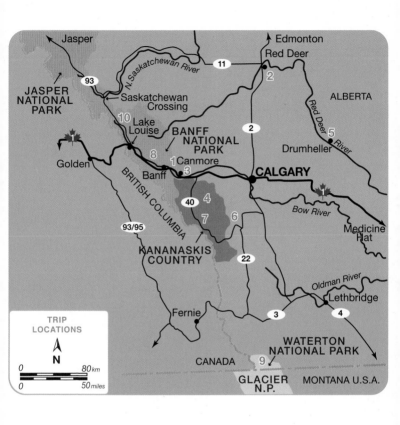

Daisies

Mt. Inglismaldie, Minnewanka Loop (Trip 1)

WOW

Your time is short, but the pavement is endless. So here you go: the ten southwest-Alberta road rides most likely to make you say "Wow!" Plus our spin-tested opinions: why we recommend each trip, what to expect, how to enjoy the optimal experience.

We hope our suggestions compel you to ride more often and keep pedaling longer. Do it because cycling is an enriching means of travel. Astride a bike, you don't just see the land, you appreciate it viscerally. Do it because cycling is a thrilling athletic pursuit. It's the closest you'll ever get to actually flying. Do it because cycling is good for you. Each time you step off your bike, you're a better person: healthier, happier, saner.

Where Exactly?

In southwest Alberta, about 80 km (50 mi) east of the Canadian Rockies' front ranges, and on the west edge of the vast prairie that girds Canada's abdomen, is a youthful metropolis pulsing with energy.

It's 244 km (151 mi) north of the imaginary line severing Canada from the U.S., and Alberta from Montana. Driving time: two-and-a-half hours via Highway 2.

It's 294 km (176 mi) south of Edmonton, the provincial capital. Driving time: three hours via Highway 2.

It's 1049 km (652 mi) east of Vancouver, British Columbia. Driving time: ten hours via Trans-Canada Highway 1.

Flight times to the city's international airport (YYC) are 80 minutes from Vancouver (YVR), three hours from Los Angeles (LAX), and less than four hours from Chicago (ORD).

Welcome to Calgary, Alberta, Canada: latitude 51° 2' 45" N, longitude 114° 3' 26" W, elevation 1048 metres (3438 ft), on the banks of the Bow River.

Ride First, Read Later

Because our emphasis here is efficient use of limited time, we don't expect you to read the rest of this introduction.

Not immediately, anyway.

We resent guidebooks that begin with a perfunctory *How To Use This Book* section. As if it were required reading. As if books were a strange, new marvel. We assume you feel the same.

We figure you'll flip to the ten premier rides, pick one and go, just as we would.

Read or ride? No contest. The greatest book of all is the earth itself. Going on a bike ride is a way of turning the pages.

But before Calgary is in your rearview mirror, keep reading. It won't take long. And what you learn will top-up your understanding of a place that's going to be on your mind a long, long time after you leave.

Wild Rose Country

Alberta is huge, roughly the size of Texas, with which it's often compared.

But other than a lot of wheat, a few cowboys, a whiff of manure, and a penchant for beef (Albertans have bumper stickers professing their bovine love), the two are more dissimilar than alike.

The population of Alberta—roughly 3,200,000—is one-sixth that of the Lone Star State.

Alberta also has way, way more oil. Each year, the province exports $7 billion worth of petrochemicals.

Global oil dominance is shifting to wild rose country, away from Saudi Arabia and the Middle East. Within a few years, Alberta will likely be the biggest single oil producer in the world.

Cascade Mountain, from Minnewanka Loop (Trip 1)

As a result, the Alberta economy has a petroleum-powered rocket strapped to its back. Business is booming. Housing construction is booming. Provincial pride is booming.

Like ants invading a picnic, workers from eastern Canada are amassing here. So many, in fact, that the jilted provinces are buying billboards in Alberta, begging the defectors to return.

Still, the Alberta money mill needs more grist. Employers are so desperate for staff, many are forced to put "closed" signs in their windows for lack of someone to take customers' cash.

So Alberta doesn't feel like Texas.

True, much of it is prairie and therefore somewhat Texan in appearance. But the focus of this book, Alberta's lower left-hand corner, looks distinctly different. That's because it's seriously mountainous, with elevations exceeding not just one but *two* Texas miles.

On this continent, the only ranges as wild and peak-studded as the Canadian Rockies, are farther north, in Alaska.

The Rockies

Peering up at Alberta's tumultuous southwest skyline, it's difficult to believe the region was once mountain-less.

About 1.5 billion years ago this was the north shore of a vast supercontinent surrounded by shallow, warm seas teeming with the earliest forms of multicellular life.

Between 140 million and 45 million years ago, two separate collisions of continental plates (moving slower than the speed of a growing fingernail) pushed up sedimentary rock—limestone, dolomite, shale, sandstone, quartz—from the ancient ocean floor. Thrust skyward, it formed the Canadian Rockies.

These peaks are the guardians of an immense wilderness. The heart of the range—an area larger than New Jersey—is protected by six contiguous national and provincial parks, where wolves,

Bighorn sheep on Lake Minnewanka loop (Trip 1)

grizzly bears, elk, caribou, bighorn sheep, mountain goats and their alpine brethren outnumber human residents.

Together, they were designated a UNESCO World Heritage Site due to their "outstanding universal value," "superlative natural phenomena," and "exceptional natural beauty and aesthetic importance."

The honour was deserved, the description accurate. This *is* an idiosyncratically beautiful cordillera.

Other ranges, blunt and cloaked in forest, are shy compared to this brazen breed. Here, the mountains are extroverts who bare their full, rock-hard musculature for all to see.

The cliffs are sheer and soaring. The summits sharp and serrated. And there seems no end to their spiky multitude. From a high vantage in Banff National Park, the horizon resembles a shark's mouth: row upon row of wicked incisors.

Mt. Inglismaldie in the Fairholme Range, mid-April (Trip 1)

Some mountains, especially volcanoes—Mt. Fuji, Mt. Kilimanjaro, Mt Rainier for example—have what appear from a distance to be relatively smooth slopes. Like the chord progression in a traditional song, they break the horizon gently, rise unbroken to a crescendo, then gradually resolve back into the horizon.

Not so the Canadian Rockies. In musical terms, these mountains are avant-garde. They've abandoned not just chord progressions, but chords, scales, and rhythmic meters in favour of improvisation.

The resulting shapes are fantastic. Infinitely varied. Jazz set in stone, lofted into the sky.

All mountains are works in progress. But more than most, the Canadian Rockies have been immortalized in their present state by humankind's favourite art form: film.

Hollywood turned its cameras on Banff National Park before moving pictures had sound. Like a burly stuntman, the range has successfully stood-in for the Swiss Alps many times.

Even the iconic, wild west that's permanently lodged between most Americans' ears is largely composed of imagery filmed in the Canadian Rockies.

The Badlands

The Rockies are visible from Calgary. The region's other defining geologic feature is just beyond view.

Climb to the top floor of the city's tallest office tower, turn away from the mountains, squint until your eyes water, and you still won't see it. But it's there, hidden below the rim of the prairie: the Canadian Badlands.

It's a sensuous dreamscape of canyons, ravines, gullies and hoodoos. It's also an arresting reminder that the seeming permanence of land and life is a cruel illusion.

Ascending out of Drumheller Valley (Trip 5)

Tyrannosaurus Rex terrorizes Drumheller.

At first sight, you'll know why an old prospector supposedly exclaimed "Something awful happened here!" upon witnessing the Grand Canyon.

A cataclysm is what created the Canadian Badlands. About 12,000 years ago, at the end of the last ice age, meltwater torrents from rapidly receding glaciers swept away soil and gouged the earth.

The result is itself a spectacle, but the erosion revealed more than subcutaneous strata. It carved through overlying sediments, down to the time of the dinosaurs, exposing their fossils.

Epic devastation like this has granted nearly all the great paleontological discoveries, for example in the Gobi Desert of China and Mongolia, and in the canyonlands of the North American West.

The Canadian Badlands, however, are unique. They're among the world's richest lodes of dinosaur bones, yet they're easier to visit than other famous dig sites.

The town of Drumheller is right there, as is the Royal Tyrrell Museum of Paleontology (www.tyrrellmuseum.com). Without a pith helmet or desert boots, you can examine mounted skeletons of 40 ancient dinosaurs.

Who named this kind of terrain "badlands"? Nearly everyone who encountered it, here and elsewhere.

The Lakota referred to it as "mako sica," and Spanish colonists called it "malpais." Both mean "bad land." French trappers called it "les mauvaises terres à traverser," which means "the bad lands to cross."

Recognizing the historical term was apt, geologists and cartographers adopted it. Badlands comprise steep slopes, loose dry soil, slick clay, and deep sand, all of which impeded travel, agriculture, and settlement.

Perpetual Boomtown

On any sunny, August day, GoBots hard at work in their gleaming, Calgary office towers can peer down and see less industrious fellow citizens tubing, kayaking, canoeing and rafting the Bow River.

11,000 years ago, the observer with the most commanding perspective would have been a raven in a riverbank cottonwood tree. What he might have seen was a pair of natives paddling down the Bow. If so, they would have been members of the Blackfoot Nation—the region's earliest known human inhabitants.

Explorer and cartographer David Thompson spent the winter of 1787 with a band of Peigan (closely related to the Blackfoot) encamped along the Bow River. He was the first European to visit the area. The initial European settlers arrived much later, in 1873.

Red Rock Parkway,
Vimy Peak beyond (Trip 9)

In 1875 the North West Mounted Police (now the RCMP) established a post near the confluence of the Bow and Elbow rivers to "protect" the western plains from American whiskey traders.

Initially called *Bow River Fort*, it was renamed *Fort Calgary* in 1876 by a Scotsman who evidently left his imagination in his homeland when he set sail for the new world.

Cattle ranching soon supplanted buffalo hunting. The Canadian Pacific Railway arrived in 1883. By the following year, the settlement had attracted a population of 4,000 and was declared a city.

Like most western burgs, it was constructed almost entirely of wood. But a devastating fire in 1886 inspired the townspeople to rebuild using the abundant local sandstone. Quarries opened and rapidly expanded. Calgary became "The Sandstone City."

In 1913 the sandstone was exhausted and Calgary's first boom sputtered. But economic salvation soon bubbled to the surface. Oil was discovered in nearby Turner Valley in 1914.

Delayed by the First World War, Calgary's second boom—the first of several stoked by petroleum—spanned the mid to late 1920s.

The Great Depression and the Second World War arrested Calgary's growth until the late 1940s, when massive oil fields were discovered in Alberta. Most were north, closer to Edmonton, yet Calgary maintained an administrative grip on the bonanza.

You'll pass picturesque farms while cycling in southwest Alberta.

A thriving agricultural industry also contributed to the city's development. Calgary grew vigourously through most of the 1950s and 60s.

The 1973 Arab Oil Embargo sent the price of petroleum to alarming new heights. It also made Calgary's previous oil booms look banal. More than 3,000 people began arriving each month.

The city accommodated the deluge by renovating and expanding at a torrid pace. Much of "The Sandstone City" was razed. Skyscrapers popped up faster than gophers on the prairie. The low-rise downtown suddenly resembled Manhattan.

With an economy precariously dependent on one industry, the city's growth peaked in 1981 along with the price of oil. The recession that gripped much of the world got its hands on Calgary in 1982.

Unemployment spread like a pox, as did office vacancies. Optimism crashed; despair flourished. Eastbound traffic surged; westbound traffic dwindled. There wasn't a U-Haul trailer left in the city.

Continued low oil prices prevented full recovery until the 1990s. But Calgary benefited hugely from a salubrious tonic at a pivotal moment: the XV Olympic Winter Games, in 1988.

The city's debut on the world stage was, by all measures, a smashing success. The event earned Calgary beaucoup profits, renewed civic self-esteem, and the high-regard of all who attended or watched it on TV.

It also bequeathed the city an invaluable structural legacy, notably the Saddledome—a 17,000-seat venue that now hosts NHL hockey games, and big-ticket concerts, rodeos, ice shows, circuses, and conventions.

The dome's architecturally distinctive, saddle-shaped roof is a Calgary icon. It elegantly symbolizes the city's western heritage and contemporary essence.

Today, the city continues juggling these two aspects of itself, trying to keep both balls—old and new—in the air at the same time. But in truth, Calgary is not what it was.

The city is home to the University of Calgary, with an enrollment of 30,000, an internationally renowned school of business, and a reputation for research leadership.

The city has an exemplary light-rail transit system—the C-Train—linking residential neighbourhoods with downtown in minutes.

The city attracts performers like Wynton Marsalis, the most prominent jazz musician of the modern era, who played to a wildly appreciative sell-out crowd.

The city is not the least bit frontier-esque. If anything, it resembles the utopian future portrayed in the famous, prime-time cartoon TV series *The Jetsons*.

Calgary's Saddledome

Yet Calgary's former self is an invaluable marketing asset—the key to differentiating it from other modern cities—so it continues trotting it out at every opportunity.

It's latest advertising slogan?

"Heart of the New West."

Carpe Diem

Calgary is Canada's fastest growing city.

Roughly 100 people move there every day, so it's impossible to state the city's precise population, but it now exceeds 1,000,000.

Calgary is Canada's youngest city.

The average age is 35. Knowing that, however, simply confirms what is visible and palpable: Calgary is as optimistic, dynamic and confident as any city on earth.

The Bow River and downtown Calgary

Calgary is Canada's best educated city.

Many Calgarians work in the sleek, 40-floor, glass-and-concrete office towers that house Canada's biggest oil and gas companies and that give the downtown skyline its distinctive, metropolis-of-tomorrow appearance.

Conspicuously clean, exceptionally prosperous, marvelously diverse, Calgary is in many ways a model of urban success.

It's beautiful, too. Compassionate city planners have blessed the citizenry with more than 21,000 acres of parkland.

And while not everyone on Easy Street is necessarily happy, there's no arguing most Calgarians have reason to smile.

Unemployment is virtually nil. Oil and gas money is gushing into the economy. The province paid off all government debt, asked the populace how it should spend its budget surplus, then sent a $400 cheque to each Albertan—just for being a resident.

Though Calgary's recent growth has been orgiastic, and its prosperity is fueled by petroleum, it was ranked *World's Cleanest City* by the Mercer Quality of Living Survey published in *Forbes Magazine*.

It was also named *10th Best City To Live In* by the Economist Intelligence Unit (www.eiu.com), which "provides a constant flow of analysis and forecasts on more than 200 countries worldwide."

In winter, however, when the mercury plummets, "quality of life" seems like a sadistic joke.

Calgary's record low temperature is -45°C (-49°F), which explains why the city has the world's most extensive skyway network (elevated, enclosed, pedestrian bridges linking buildings) and the world's largest expanse of indoor urban greenery: the Devonian Gardens (4th Floor, TD Square).

Yet Calgarians rarely express resentment of their harsh winters. They're not repressed by months of frigid weather. Just the opposite. They embrace the cold and snow: time to go skiing, boarding, ice skating.

Come spring, however, when the sun finally pierces the arctic chill, you can feel the tension burst. Calgarians' lusty appetite for summer belies their creatures-of-the-ice stoicism.

They begin celebrating early. And each year, their list of festivals grows longer. It's now approaching 50. These are among the most popular:

> Independent Film Festival (March)
> FunnyFest Comedy Festival (April)
> International Children's Festival (May)
> Lilac Festival (May)
> Mosaic Cultural Festival (June)
> CariFest (Caribbean culture, June)
> International Jazz Festival (June)
> Greek Festival (June)
> Fiestaval (Latin Culture, July)

Sculptures near Olympic Plaza, downtown Calgary

Calgary Stampede (July)
Folk Music Festival (July)
Afrikadey! (African culture, August)
GlobalFest (cultural diversity, August)
Fringe Festival (theatre, August)
Taste of Calgary (local cuisine, August)
International Reggae Festival (August)
International Blues Festival (August)
International Film Festival (September)

The big one, of course, is the Calgary Stampede—a 10-day event with a nearly 100-year history. Attendance has recently exceeded 1.26 million. Another couple million watch it on TV.

The heart of the event is the world's largest outdoor rodeo. Swirling around it are chuckwagon races, a sprawling agricultural fair, Las Vegas-style casinos, concerts by country-music stars, and a whopping parade that shuts the city down for an entire day.

Plateau above Drumheller Valley (Trip 5)

To see au courant Calgary pretend it's just an old-fashioned cowtown is hilarious. Offices fortify their entrances with bales of hay. Banks disguise themselves as corrals. Hotels turn their ballrooms into saloons. And corporate-sponsored pancake breakfasts—free to the public—spill onto sidewalks and into parking lots.

As a result, the Stampede is a raucous street-party á la Mardi Gras, but with a lot less flesh and infinitely more ten-gallon hats. Many Calgarians swap their power suits for boots, jeans and neckerchiefs, then swagger (or stagger) about, practicing their one-word cowboy vocabularies: "Yeehaa!"

When the party's over, Calgary immediately sobers up and gets back to business. But nobody takes the long-awaited, hard-earned summer for granted.

On the solstice (June 21), the sun rises at 5:21 a.m. and sets at 9:53 p.m. That's 16.5 hours of daylight. And Calgarians exploit it with the same enthusiasm they do the other natural treasures in their resource-rich province.

Whether it's oil or sunshine, their prevailing attitude is "Carpe diem."

Après-spin

Near Fort McMurray, about 756 km (470 mi) north of Calgary, industrial battalions are frantically teasing oil out of tarry black sand—enough to make their province the biggest petroleum supplier to the United States.

Their unceasing toil generates truckloads of money, most of which funnels through Calgary, where it's created a demand for, and thus a supply of, innumerable indulgences.

For cyclists, who are inevitably famished, this means the post-ride meal can be nearly as much of an event as the ride itself.

Calgary offers a selection of restaurants whose chefs (and prices) vie with those in Toronto or Montreal, and scores of eateries serving generous helpings of delicious if not gourmet fare at reasonable prices.

Given the reputation of Alberta beef (prized as far away as Karachi, capital of Pakistan), it's natural to assume Calgary's cuisine is laden with big slabs of grilled sirloin. And that's partly correct: superior steakhouses abound.

Walk down Stephen Avenue (the 8th Avenue pedestrian mall between 1st and 6th streets SW, where a clutch of historical, honey-hued, sandstone buildings remain) and you'll find Saltlik Steakhouse (403-537-1160), reputed to be among the city's best. Nearby is the Metropolitan Grill (403-263-5432), another local favourite for AAA Alberta beef.

But cowboy vittles represent only a small slice of Calgary's delectable culinary pie.

Stephen Avenue

When Canada was building its transcontinental railway, many workers laying track on the westbound crew were Chinese. Those who settled in Calgary created a vibrant Chinatown, now crowded with restaurants. And the train itself brought subsequent waves of immigrants whose cuisine lends international spice to the city's menus.

Try Falafel King (803 1st Street SW, 403-269-KING) for a quick-but-hearty meal. Try Marathon (130 10th Street NW, 403-283 6796) for an Ethiopian feast. Try Open Sesame (6920 MacLeod Trail SE, 403-259-0123) for a spicy stir-fry in an exotic, Asian atmosphere. Try the Conga Room (109 8th Avenue SW, 403-262-7248) for nuevo Latino food in a Habana Vieja setting. Try Kim Anh (626 17th Avenue SW, 403-228-2380) for bánh mì—a Vietnamese submarine sandwich.

Aiming uptown? Rouge (1240 8th Avenue SE, 403-531-2767) is a romantic French restaurant in a historic Kensington-neighbourhood house. The Vintage Chophouse and Tavern (322 11th Avenue SW, 403-262-7262) has 300 wines in their cellar and live blues and jazz on stage each weekend. Capo (1420 9th Avenue SE, 403-264-2276) in Inglewood is the city's primo Italiano ristorante. Catch (100 8th Avenue SE, 403-206-0000) serves seafood caught that morning on both coasts.

Want to make your own? Swing into Community Natural Foods (1304 10th Avenue SW, 403-229-2383) then take your fresh, nutritious, picnic fixin's to Prince's Island Park, wedged between downtown and the Bow River, just north of the Eau Claire district.

All you want is a good cup of joe? Calgary is thoroughly caffeinated, so your options are dizzying. One standout is Higher Grounds Cafe (403-270-3780), a bustling independent coffee shop in Kensington—the city's bohemian strolling-and-shopping district, just across the Louise Bridge from downtown.

What? You're still hankerin' for western grub? Alright, you asked for it. Go to Buzzards (140 10th Avenue SW, 403-264-6959). Order the prairie oysters: bull testicles breaded in crackers and fried in butter. You haven't eaten the cowboy way until you've popped a few of these jewels into your mouth.

Once your appetite is sated, feed your soul. It's easy to do in Calgary, because the arts are flourishing, as they always do wherever the financial tide rises.

Having completed a graceful jeté past its 40th anniversary season, the Alberta Ballet (www.albertaballet.com) is led by choreographer Jean Grand-Maître, who created works for the most acclaimed companies in Europe before coming to Calgary.

The Calgary Philharmonic Orchestra (www.cpo-live.com) has been soothing the city since 1955. Today it presents about five concerts each month, including midweek lunchtime and Saturday morning performances. The illustrious music director is Roberto Minczuk, formerly with the New York Philharmonic.

Teatro restaurant patio on Olympic Plaza

With more than 34 crystal-shattering seasons behind it, the Calgary Opera (www.calgaryopera.com) consistently attracts near-capacity audiences. In its '06-'07 season, it presented three world premieres, two Canadian premieres, and several company premieres.

The Epcor Centre for the Performing Arts (205 8th Avenue SE, www.epcorcentre.org, 403-294-7444) occupies an entire city block. Each year it sells more than 300,000 tickets to some 1800 performances including live theatre, dance, and concerts spanning the symphony-jazz-folk-blues-world-rock spectrum.

The Glenbow Museum (130 9th Avenue SE, www.glenbow.org, 403-268-4100) is among Canada's most impressive. It boasts a million artifacts and 28,000 works of art. An enormous gallery is devoted to the modern history of Alberta. Another is dedicated to the province's original inhabitants, the Blackfoot Indians.

The movie theatres where you're most likely to catch a stimulating documentary or the latest indie film are the Plaza

(1133 Kensington Road NW, 403-283-3636), the Globe (617 8th Avenue SW, 403-262-3308), and the Uptown (612 8th Avenue SW, 403-265-0120).

Calgary Climate

Calgary has a semi-arid, highland continental climate strongly influenced by the nearby Rocky Mountains. Summers are short and warm. Winters are long, dry, but variable.

The daily average temperature in July is 16°C (61°F). Perhaps four days each summer, the temperature will eek past 30°C (86°F). But even on hot days, Calgary's high elevation (1048 m / 3438 ft) and low relative humidity (about 45% in summer) ensure cool evenings. Summer lows average 8°C (46°F).

Calgary is among the sunniest of Canadian cities. Sunshine is so constant that prolonged absences are rare and strike locals as odd. The corollary, of course, is that annual precipitation is scant: 301 mm (11.9 in) of rain, 112 cm (44 in) of snow.

June tends to be the city's wettest month. But precipitation decreases markedly from west to east, so the city's treed western outskirts give way to treeless grassland beyond the eastern city limit.

Each summer, there are about 20 thunderstorms in the Calgary region. It's on the edge of Alberta's "hailstorm alley," so those ominous, black clouds often unleash a barrage of icy projectiles.

You won't be cycling for pleasure here in winter (will you?), but learning more about the flipside to Calgary's mild summers might interest you, especially if you live elsewhere.

On about half of all winter days, the temperature remains below freezing (0°C / 32°F). The mercury drops past -30°C (-22°F) about five days each winter, although spells of extreme cold don't persist beyond one or two weeks.

Rosebud Creek, near Wayne (Trip 5)

While "bitterly cold" is a politely accurate description of the season, two factors make it bearable. First, the relative humidity is low (about 55% in winter), so the cold doesn't *feel* as bone chilling as it would in moister climes. Second, strong winds, warmed while rising over the Rockies, are frequent.

These windy spells are called *Chinooks*. Because they provide instant relief from winter—raising the temperature as much as 15°C (27°F) within a few hours, and lasting several days, a week, sometimes longer—Calgarians think they're heaven sent.

Chinooks are reliable, too. In the past century, only a single month in one winter (January, 1950) was Chinook-less.

Beyond the City Limits

Calgary has an impressive network of pathways and bike lanes that encourage two-wheeled transportation and recreation. So

Comparing the merits of carbon fibre and pig iron.

why isn't an inner-city ride included among this book's ten premier trips?

Our intention isn't to discourage you from biking within Calgary. It's to encourage you to explore beyond the city limits.

For umpteen obvious reasons (quick summary: health, environment, quality of life, sustainability) every city on the planet needs to construct bike paths and promote cycling.

But most cities have not done so. Nor will they, until relentlessly pestered, badgered, and hounded by citizens.

For citizens to care that much about cycling, they have to love it. To fall in love with it, they need to cycle where the experience is most joyful. And that's not within earshot of a city's roar, within close range of perpetual automobile traffic, or within constant view of buildings.

Cycling can be pleasant, practical and convenient in a city, as it certainly is in Calgary. But it's unlikely to elicit the joy, the relaxation, the thrill of cycling where nature, not urban turmoil, prevails.

So to rank Calgary's bike paths among the area's ten premier cycling routes would be an exaggeration. And it wouldn't necessarily promote the construction and use of inner-city bike paths more effectively than would pointing you toward more scenic and exhilarating routes, as we've done here.

Besides, we're confident you'll avail yourself of Calgary's acclaimed, bike-friendly nature without us urging you to do so.

Maps

The maps we created and that accompany each trip in this book are for general orientation only. Our route directions are elaborate and precise, so referring to other maps shouldn't be necessary.

But if you want a more detailed map, we recommend one in the stats box for each trip. Most are published by Gem Trek (maps@gemtrek.com). You can purchase them via mail-order from Map Town in Calgary (www.maptown.com, 877-921-6277). They're also available at outdoor shops and bookstores throughout Alberta.

Minimum Daily Requirement

Wear a helmet, sunglasses, short-sleeve jersey, and cycling-specific shorts, shoes and gloves. That plus a little sunscreen might be all you need to wear on a warm, sunny day. But if it gets breezy or cloudy, you'll want extra layers: tights, warm gloves, an insulating long-sleeve jersey, a wind shell, maybe a neck gaiter or head band. Always carry a small repair kit and a pump, so you can make adjustments and fix a flat. Your gear, plus lunch and some high-energy snacks, should fit in your seat wedge, daypack, or rack trunk. Be sure to fill your water bottles or hydration pack.

Approaching the end of Elbow Falls trail (Trip 4)

North Saskatchewan River Valley, just northwest of The Crossing,
on the Icefields Parkway (Trip 10). Mt. Wilson at the end, far left.

done in a day

the rides

trip 1
⊕ lake minnewanka

route	paved backroad
location	1¼ hours west of Calgary, in Banff National Park, northeast of Banff townsite
distance	15.5 km (9.6 mi), plus options up to 66 km (41 mi)
elevation gain	142 m (466 ft), more depending on options
cycling time	1½ hours, plus options up to 6 hours
difficulty	easy to challenging
map	Gem Trek *Banff Up-Close*

opinion

Remember your first pair of skis? Probably not. Your first ice skates? Unlikely. Your first tennis racket? Baseball glove? Soccer ball? Of course not. But your first bicycle? Absolutely, because bicycling was your first taste of freedom.

You went ripping down hill, grinning, whooping with joy. No one could stop you. For the first time, you were master of your fate. You could go anywhere you wanted, or at least it seemed so.

That's why bicycles are time machines. Jump on a bike and, regardless of your age, suddenly you're twelve again: light, fast, utterly free, flying into a world of promise. And that's why a bike trip, especially in spring, is rejuvenating.

Calgarians have lots of places to ride. A few are optimal in spring—enhanced by mountain scenery and temporarily closed to motorists. One of the best is the Lake Minnewanka loop, near Banff townsite.

Entirely paved, it's ideal for road bikes or hybrids. Mountain bikers ride it too, though pedaling knobby tires on pavement

*Mt. Inglismaldie in the Fairholme Range,
above Lake Minnewanka, mid-April*

is labourious. Until April 15, a barricaded 5-km (3.1-mi) stretch liberates you from vehicles and ensures minimal traffic the rest of the way.

Lacking monster hills yet affording a long, swift descent, the loop is short enough for kids, merciful on winter-weakened muscles, and easily lengthened into a challenging trip.

The city bike path is fine. But for your spring inaugural ride? Go cycling in Canada's premier national park.

fact

before your trip

To see the Banff National Park entry-fee schedule prior to arriving at the park gate, visit www.pc.gc.ca/pn-np/ab/banff, click on "visitor information," then click on "fees."

The Palliser Range above Lake Minnewanka

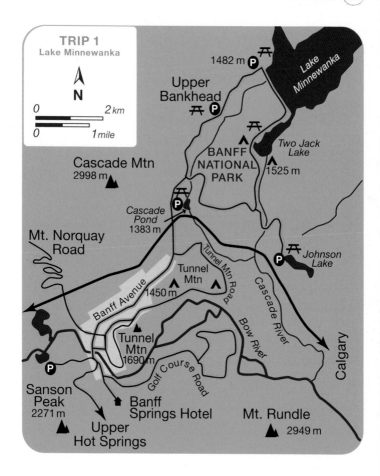

TRIP 1
Lake Minnewanka

N

0 ——— 2 km
0 ——— 1 mile

Lake Minnewanka

1482 m P 🏕

Upper
Bankhead 🏕 P

Cascade Mtn
2998 m ▲

BANFF
NATIONAL
PARK

Two Jack
Lake

🏕 1525 m

Cascade
Pond
1383 m P

Mt. Norquay
Road

🏕 P Johnson
Lake

Tunnel Mtn Road

Banff Avenue

Tunnel
Mtn
1450 m

Cascade River

Bow River

Calgary

P

Sanson
Peak
2271 m

Tunnel
Mtn
1690 m

Golf Course Road

Banff
Springs Hotel

Mt. Rundle
2949 m ▲

Upper
Hot Springs

getting there

From Calgary, drive Hwy 1 west, past Canmore. Proceed north-west into Banff National Park. Take the first Banff townsite exit (right), also signed for Lake Minnewanka. Turn right (north) onto Lake Minnewanka Road. Just 0.5 km (0.3 mi) farther, turn right (east) into Cascade Pond picnic area, at 1383 m (4537 ft).

Mt. Inglismaldie

the ride

From the parking lot, return to **Lake Minnewanka Road**. Go right. In 0.5 km (0.3 mi) reach a junction. You can go either way, but proceed straight (northeast) to ride the loop clockwise and enjoy the easiest ascent and sharpest descent.

Immediately beyond the junction, the road is barricaded November 15 through April 14, preventing motorists from accessing Lake Minnewanka this way and allowing animals to feed undisturbed by vehicle traffic. It's still closed? All the better. Push your bike beyond the barricade and resume pedaling.

Just before passing **Upper Bankhead Day Use Area**, you might encounter a short stretch of snow-covered road in the shadow of Cascade Mountain. On a road bike, you'll want to dismount and walk through. Mountain bikers might be able to keep riding.

From Cascade Pond, it's a gradual 6-km (3.7-mi) climb to a parking lot at 1482 m (4862 ft), just above **Lake Minnewanka's west shore**. Push your bike past the other barricade here. Beyond, you'll rejoin vehicle traffic, but it's generally light.

Banff Springs Hotel and the Bow River, from Tunnel Mountain Road

Ahead (east-northeast), past the boat dock, is a spacious picnic area with three shelters. To continue the loop, turn right (south-east) and cross the **dam**. Minnewanka is Banff Park's largest lake. It's in view here, as are many of the surrounding peaks.

Past the dam, the road curves right and ascends. Bighorn sheep often congregate here. Soon pass **Two Jack Lake** and crest the loop's 1525-m (5003-ft) highpoint. Reach a junction at 11.5 km (7.1 mi). To continue the loop, bear right (south). Left descends southeast to forest-ringed **Johnson Lake**. If you're feeling strong, it's a worthwhile 4.5-km (2.8-mi) detour. The 75-m (246-ft) downhill is fun, but it's uphill all the way back.

Resuming the loop from the 11.5-km (7.1-mi) junction, soon attain a grand view of Cascade Mountain (west) and careen through a swooping 100-m (328-ft) descent. Just past the over-flow camping area, reach the junction where you slipped past the **first barricade**.

You're now on familiar ground. Turn left (southwest) to reach **Cascade Pond** and complete the 15.5-km (9.6-mi) loop. But you don't have to stop here. Ride the loop again, or continue cycling around Tunnel Mountain—a 15-km (9.3-mi) loop closer to Banff townsite.

For Tunnel Mountain, keep pedaling straight (south) on Lake Minnewanka Road. Proceed beneath the highway overpass. About 1 km farther, turn left (east) onto Tunnel Mountain Road and begin a gentle ascent.

Near the road's 1450-m (4757-ft) highpoint, stop to overlook the **hoodoos**. Then cruise west, above the Bow River and past the campground. Where Tunnel Mountain Road continues straight, turn left (south) on Tunnel Mountain Scenic Drive.

Coast south, stopping above the confluence of the Spray and Bow rivers to peer down at **Bow Falls**. The road then veers right (northwest), descending onto Buffalo Street in downtown Banff and soon intersecting **Banff Avenue**.

Decision time. If you've had enough, turn right (north) to pierce the town and exit it northeast. After ducking beneath the highway, arrive at your vehicle parked near Cascade Pond. If you want more, take your pick:

(1) Roam the quieter **residential streets** of Banff townsite.

(2) Turn left (south) onto Banff Avenue, cross the Bow River, turn left onto Spray Avenue, turn left onto Bow Falls Drive, cross the Spray River, then continue onto **Golf Course Road** (closed until May) where you can ride an 11-km (6.8-mi) circuit beneath Mt. Rundle.

(3) Turn left (south) onto Banff Avenue, cross the Bow River, turn left onto Spray Avenue, turn right onto Mountain Avenue, ascend 217 m (712 ft) in 3.3 km (2.1 mi) to the **Upper Hot Springs** at 1600 m (5249 ft), then plummet back into town.

(4) Cross Banff Avenue, turn right onto Bear Street, continue north on Lynx and Gopher streets, cross the railway and highway, then proceed toward **Mt. Norquay**, climbing 317 m (1040 ft) in 5.6 km (3.5 mi) to the ski area at 1700 m (5577 ft), then hurtling back into town.

trip 2
⊕ waskasoo park

route	paved bicycle paths
location	1½ hours north of Calgary, in Red Deer
distance	30 km (18.6 mi) or more
elevation gain	80 m (262 ft)
cycling time	2½ to 3 hours
difficulty	easy
map	pathway map available at Kerry Wood Nature Centre

opinion

Red Deer is remarkably Dutch in its respect for cycling.

Since touring Holland by bike a few years ago, Red Deer is the first place we've ridden that reminded us of the land where city planners acknowledge bicycles are as important as automobiles.

Red Deer has 200 km (124 mi) of paved cycling paths. Yet its population is just 90,000.

Compare that to Calgary, whose paths are 1½ times longer but whose population is twelve times greater. Calgary is often cited as the promised land for urban cyclists. Relative to city size, however, Red Deer's pathway system is far more impressive.

The Red Deer system also lacks the tacked-on, afterthought, patched-together feel that degrades the cycling experience on most urban pathways.

From the seat of a bike, it's easy to imagine the pioneering founders built the pathway first, then let the city grow up around it.

Yet it's not the metropolis you primarily see as you pedal the pathway's main arteries. It's leafy, grassy, river-and-creek laced parkland.

The Red Deer map looks like it was painted by a green-obsessed Jackson Pollock: it's streaked and splattered with parks. And the pathway links most of them.

Following the Red Deer River, the path weaves along the water's edge, darts into forests, climbs to a cliffside viewpoint, then swoops back to the riverbank.

Along Waskasoo and Piper creeks, the path jumps playfully back and forth across the water via small, arching, wooden bridges built solely for pedestrians and cyclists, like those that lend a fairytale aura to Holland's famously car-free village of Geithorn.

Near the pathway's north end, you'll wind through the Kerry Wood Nature Centre, near Gaetz Lake. Established in 1924, it comprises Alberta's first federal migratory bird sanctuary.

The Centre is the ideal place to begin your Red Deer bicycle tour, because it has a spacious parking lot, shaded picnic tables, public toilets, and a helpful staff.

It's open daily 10 a.m. to 8 p.m., and 1 p.m. to 5 p.m. on holidays. Pick up a pathway map there for under $2. Then devise your own route, or ride the heart of the system described below.

fact

getting there

From Calgary, drive Highway 2 north. Take exit 401 to enter Red Deer on 67th Street. Turn right (south) on Gaetz Avenue, left (east) on 55th Street, then left (north) on 45th Avenue. The Kerry Wood Nature Centre is at 6300 45th Avenue, 1.5 km (0.9 mi) north of 55th Street. The elevation here is 860 m (2822 ft.)

Piper Creek bridge

the ride

Stepping out of the Kerry Wood Nature Centre, right is north. Begin cycling in that direction, through the parking lot, onto the **McKenzie Trail**.

Ride beneath the bridge, turn right (west), ascend onto the bridge, then bear right (east) to cross the **Red Deer River**. On the far side of the bridge, turn right and descend, following the sign for Lions Campground.

Cross the road to the riverside bike path. Bear right (south) to follow it upstream. The path quickly departs the road and plunges into riverside greenery.

Past the campground, reach a 4-way junction. A former **CPR bridge** built in 1907 spans the river to your left. Proceed straight (southwest). Pass beneath the Taylor Road bridge.

Cow parsnip

77th St

2

Taylor Drive

67th St

Waskasoo
Park
Red Deer

Bower
Pond

Red Deer
Golf Club

Heritage Ranch

Calgary

TRIP 2
Waskasoo Park

N

0   1 km

0   0.5 mile

3-mile
Bend
Rec
Area

shale trail

Gaetz (50th) Ave

Kerry Wood
Nature Centre
860 m

Red Deer River

45th Ave

55th St

48th Ave

downtown Red Deer

48th St

Barrett Park

Rotary
Park

Westerner Park

Red Deer River

After skirting **Bower Pond**, which has a fountain in it, cross a wooden bridge and go left. Cycle among big trees, then along the river again.

A bridge conveys you across the river, into **Heritage Ranch**. Bear left past a windmill and an inviting covered picnic shelter.

Heading south, between the forest (left) and Highway 2 (right), ignore the right fork vaulting over a bridge. Go left and curve behind the **horse corrals**.

Beyond the parking lot, go left (east) onto the path paralleling **Cronquist Drive**. It soon curves left and passes a viewpoint above the river.

Pedal along the bluff, then coast downhill. But before the path levels, turn sharply left onto the signed **South Bank Trail**.

You're now cycling generally northeast, following the river downstream. Pass beneath four bridges. Immediately after the fourth, ignore an unsigned right fork.

Red Deer's Waskasoo Park

Cross a bridged creek, ascend abruptly, then fork right (south). But note this junction. You'll return here later. When you do, you'll fork the other way, along the river.

For now, ride south, away from the river. The path ahead briefly merges with streets, so pay closer attention.

Cross a stoplight and ride through a short alley. Go left on 52nd Street to regain the path. It quickly forks. Go right to proceed south through **Barrett Park**.

Cross 48th Avenue to enter **Rotary Park**. Follow the path left, between the park and the parking lot. It ascends beside

One of numerous pathway bridges in Waskasoo Park

48th, then veers right (south), dives into forest and crosses a wooden bridge.

After passing the beige cement-block toilet building, fork right. Cycle south through **Bower Woods**, over more wooden bridges, and beside a playground and fountain.

Pierce a cement underpass to enter more forest. It seems you're deep in nature here. Then the path suddenly pops out of a ravine to reveal an alarming sight: Zellers.

Parallel residential Barrett Drive for a short distance to 19th Street, where you'll see **Westerner Park** and the Red Deer Centrium.

The path ends here, so the Zellers sign is actually a warning. It means "Turn around. Go back to the forest."

Retrace your route north to the junction where you previously departed the Red Deer River. Bear right (northeast). Then go left at the next junction to reach the Kerry Wood Nature Centre.

trip 3

tour de canmore

route	paved byways and neighbourhood streets
location	45 minutes west of Calgary, in the Bow River Valley
distance	40 km (25 mi) or more
elevation gain	300 m (984 ft) or more
cycling time	2 to 3 hours or more
difficulty	moderate
map	Gem Trek *Best of Canmore*, or free Town of Canmore map available at Rebound Cycle

opinion

Like satellite dishes precisely positioned for optimal reception, Canmore's posh chalets are aimed at the Three Sisters, so the image of this striking alpine trinity comes beaming in through their cathedral windows.

But the way to really appreciate this flourishing mountain village isn't by sitting in an overstuffed chair and staring in one direction. It's by riding your bike.

Cycling allows you to admire not just the Sisters, but all the pinnacles ringing the town as you swoop along the flanks of Mount Rundle, Ha Ling Peak, and Mount Lady Macdonald.

You can also play architecture critic while pedaling past multi-million-dollar alpine-style castles—now as profuse as wildflowers along the mountains' lower slopes.

Only on a road bike can you take full pleasure in cruising the paved streets, though a mountain bike will suffice. Canmore

Grotto Mountain, from Palliser Trail

has a few short bike paths, but none allow the speeds that competent road bikers maintain. Stick to the streets.

The routes described below comprise boulevards wide enough to be safe for cyclists. On none will you feel badgered by motorists, because traffic is generally light.

Is there really enough road riding in and around Canmore to keep you spinning for a few hours? Yes. Even if you ride at an athletic pace. Hills are frequent and steep, too, so expect to work up an appetite.

That could be the best reason of all to spend an afternoon touring Canmore by bike. The town's growing affluence has spawned several superb restaurants.

For a meal as distinctive as your day in the saddle, try Quarry Bistro (678-6088, www.quarrybistro.com) at 718 Main Street.

Seated on Quarry's sidewalk patio or near the windows, you can feel the pulse of downtown and see the mountains, so it's

Returning to Canmore from Harvie Heights. The Three Sisters are beyond (right).

as if you're still exploring Canmore—with your palate instead of your pedals.

Their French and Italian bistro fare emphasizes fresh, local, organic produce and is occasionally garnished with rare, bear's tooth mushrooms gathered by a Bow Valley wildcrafter.

Quarry is owned and run by a sister-and-brother team: Naomi and David Wyse. Given 24 hours notice they'll serve you a chef's tasting menu—a delectable tour de Quarry.

fact

getting there

From Calgary, drive Highway 1 west. Take the downtown Canmore exit.

After curving right over the highway, cross Bow Valley Trail and the railroad tracks. Turn left onto Main Street. Proceed to 8th Avenue and turn left. Follow it over the Bow River bridge.

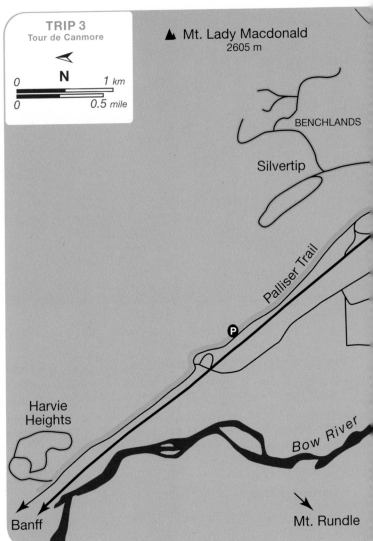

TRIP 3
Tour de Canmore

N

0 ____ 1 km
0 ____ 0.5 mile

▲ Mt. Lady Macdonald
2605 m

BENCHLANDS

Silvertip

Palliser Trail

P

Harvie Heights

Bow River

Banff

Mt. Rundle

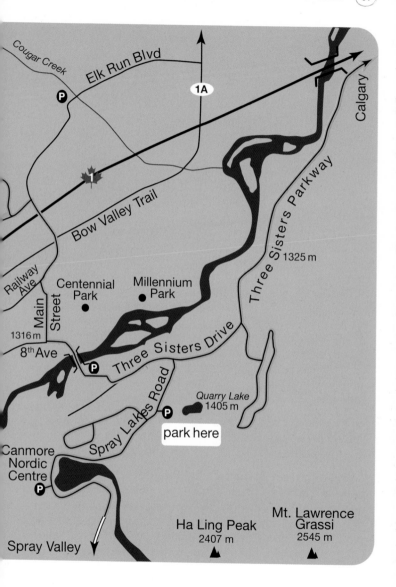

Cruising downtown Canmore

At the T-junction, turn left onto Three Sisters Drive. Ascend, forking right onto Spray Lakes Road. Shortly beyond, turn left into the Quarry Lake parking lot, at 1405 m (4610 ft).

the ride

Pick up a free Canmore map at the town's premier bike shop: Rebound Cycle, at 8th Avenue and Main Street. After trying these initial suggestions, let curiosity and impulse guide you.

7-km (4.3-mi) circuit beneath Mt. Rundle

Exit the Quarry Lake parking lot, turn left onto Spray Lakes Road and pedal northwest. Proceed straight where Rundleview Drive forks right. Mt. Rundle is visible ahead. After a gradual ascent, pass the reservoir and enjoy views of the Fairholme Range across the valley. Pass the Nordic Centre entrance.

Proceed along the reservoir, beneath Mt. Rundle's south summit, then ascend to where pavement ends. Turn around and begin a swift descent, but slow down and turn left onto Run-dleview Drive. Bear left again, loop around Evergreen Circle, then return to Spray Lakes Road.

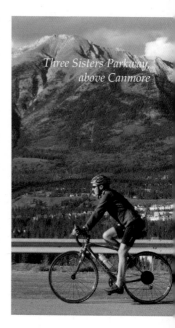

Three Sisters Parkway, above Canmore

11-km (6.8-mi) round trip on Three Sisters Parkway

From the Quarry Lake parking lot entrance, go right (southeast). Coast to the intersection then bear right (south) onto Three Sisters Drive. At the four-way stop, turn left onto Three Sisters Parkway. Follow it east then southeast to Three Sisters Village. Turn right onto Dyrgas Drive, ascend to Miscow Circle, loop through the neighbourhood, then descend to the parkway and return to Spray Lakes Road.

22-km (13.6-mi) Harvie Heights / Silvertip circuit

From the junction of Spray Lakes Road and Three Sisters Drive, descend north into town. Go right on Rundle Drive, cross the Bow River bridge, and continue north on 8th Avenue. Turn right (east) onto Main Street. At the T-junction with Railroad Avenue, turn right. Cross Bow Valley Trail and ascend over the Trans-Canada Highway. On the far side of the overpass, turn left (northwest) onto Palliser Trail, which parallels the highway.

Pass Sheraton Four Points and Silvertip Trail. Ride the Palliser Trail shoulder past the highway on-ramp, then veer right onto the bike path. Proceed northwest 4 km (2.5 mi) to Harvie Heights. Ascend right on Blue Jay Drive and loop through this peaceful, wooded hamlet. While returning to Canmore, detour left onto Silvertip Trail. Ascend steeply, turn left onto Blue Grouse Ridge, ascend to Little Ravine Road, turn right, and coast down to Silvertip Trail. Then ascend left, explore Silvertip's upper tentacles, then zip back down to Palliser Trail.

trip 4

⊕ elbow river valley

route	paved Highway 66
location	30 minutes west of Calgary, in Kananaskis Country, southwest of Bragg Creek
round trip	32 km (20 mi) from Station Flats 60 km (37.3 mi) from Bragg Creek
elevation gain	500 m (1640 ft) from Bragg Creek
cycling time	1½ to 3 hours
difficulty	easy
map	Gem Trek *Bragg Creek and Elbow Falls* or *Bragg Creek and Sheep Valley— Kananaskis Country*

opinion

Pedal at the pace of the average cyclist, and sixteen kilometers takes less than an hour to dispatch.

But if you're piercing the front range of the spectacular Rockies on a highway closed to motorists, it'll be a liberating, exhilarating hour.

That's what awaits you on Highway 66, southwest of Bragg Creek. Until May 15, you'll enjoy a rare treat: dominion over the final stretch of road. Not a car in sight. Not even a car within earshot.

The left lane affords better views? Swerve on over. Waiting for your companions to catch up? Pedal lazy circles in the middle of the road. Coasting downhill? Swoop like a skier, back and forth across the asphalt's full width.

West through Elbow River Valley to the Front Range, on Highway 66

For one intoxicating hour, you and your fellow cyclists are the grand pooh-bahs of the pavement.

Moderately strong riders begin a 60-km (37.3-mi) round trip at Bragg Creek. Starting farther southwest at Station Flats shortens it to a 32-km (20-mi) round trip. Either way, you'll initially share the highway with motorists, but it's relatively safe: broad, straight, with wide shoulders.

Families with pre-teen kids saddle up at the closed gate, riding only the vehicle-free section—a 16-km (10-mi) round trip. But they immediately ascend to Rainy Summit, the only big climb on the route.

Other than the summit, and a minor hill just before Elbow Falls, the cycling is easy. You can relax and gaze at the forested foothills. Places to stop and rest are plentiful, but the most scenic is where the highway grazes the Elbow River beyond the summit.

Elbow Falls Trail and the Rockies beyond

Unless a rogue storm sweeps through, the highway is usually snow-free by mid-April, all the way to where pavement peters out in Little Elbow Recreation Area. That allows cyclists a full month to enjoy being road hogs once they duck beneath the winter gate.

fact

getting there

Drive west out of Calgary on Highway 1, then follow Highway 22 south past the intersection with Highway 8. Or drive west out of Calgary on Highway 8, then turn left (south) onto Highway 22.

From either approach, drive Highway 22 southwest to Bragg Creek. In the village, turn right (west) at the gas station. Park in the shopping centre just beyond. The elevation here is 1300 m (4265 ft).

*Elbow Falls Trail descends from
Rainy Pass Summit,
skirting Powderface Ridge*

For a shorter bike ride, don't park at Bragg Creek. Continue
left (south) on Highway 22. At the T-junction, turn right (west)
onto Highway 66. Follow it southwest about 10 km (6.2 mi),
then turn right into the Station Flats picnic area parking lot.

the ride

Depart the east side of the Bragg Creek shopping centre.
Return to the junction in front of the gas station. Turn right
(south) then right again (southwest) onto **Highway 758**. It's
narrow and winding, so be alert for vehicles.

After briefly following the river, the highway enters Bragg
Creek Provincial Park, curves left (south), and ascends. At 5.5
km (3.4 mi) reach a T-junction. Turn right (west) onto broader,
safer, Highway 66, also known as Elbow Falls Trail.

You'll remain on **Highway 66**, traveling generally southwest,
for the rest of the ride. Views of the forested river valley and
surrounding foothills are constant.

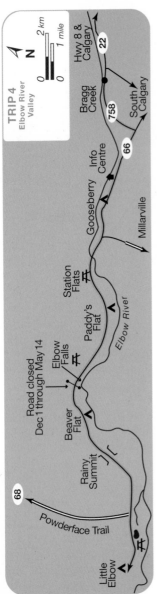

TRIP 4
Elbow River Valley

N

0   2 km
0   1 mile

Hwy 8 & Calgary

22

Bragg Creek

758

South Calgary

66

Gooseberry Info Centre

Millarville

Station Flats

Paddy's Flat

Elbow River

Road closed Dec 1 through May 14

Elbow Falls

Beaver Flat

Rainy Summit

68

Powderface Trail

Little Elbow

At 9 km (5.6 mi) pass Elbow Valley Visitor Info Centre (right). At 14 km (8.7 mi) pass **Station Flats picnic area** (right), where cyclists preferring a shorter, 32-km (20-mi) round trip should start pedaling. Several mountain-bike trails also begin here.

Though the highway is fast approaching the mountains, the riding remains easy. At 17 km (10.6 mi) pass **Paddy's Flat Recreation Area** (left), where a 3.6-km (2.2-mi) riverside hiking trail begins.

After a brief ascent and descent, reach **Elbow Falls Recreation Area** at 22 km (13.7 mi). The road is gated here, closed to motorists December 1 through May 14, granting cyclists supremacy in early spring.

The rec area harbours a popular riverbank picnic site. Families flock here on spring weekends, their parked cars lining the highway far east of the winter gate.

Beyond the gate, begin climbing in earnest. The highway gains 275 m (902 ft) in the next 4 km (2.5 mi) to 1750-m (5741-ft) **Rainy Summit**.

Elbow River Falls

Catch your breath on the crest while gazing at impressive peaks to the south including 2330-m (7644-ft) Forgetmenot Mountain.

From the summit, coast to a junction with the unpaved **Powderface Trail**. Turn left (southwest) to continue on deteriorating pavement. Soon pass Forgetmenot Pond (left).

Cycling on skinny tires you'll want to turn around at 30 km (18.6 mi), where pavement ends in **Little Elbow Recreation Area**. On fat tires you can continue, either roaming the campground or probing the Little or Big Elbow trails.

Bluebell in the forest along Elbow Falls Trail

trip 5

drumheller

route	paved Highway 10X and the Dinosaur Trail loop road
location	1½ hours northeast of Calgary, in the Drumheller Valley
round trip	30 km (18.7 mi) to Wayne 50 km (31 mi) on Dinosaur Trail loop
elevation gain	negligible to Wayne, 160 m (525 ft) on the loop
cycling time	1¼ hours for Wayne, 2½ hours for the loop
difficulty	easy to Wayne, moderate on the loop
map	Visit www.dinosaurvalley.com for a free download. Choose "Visiting Drumheller," then click on "Travel Guide" or "Maps."

opinion

Until you can vacation on distant planets, there's always the Drumheller Valley—a land as otherworldly as it gets without requiring a space suit to step out of your vehicle.

First time visitors from Calgary strain to believe this bizarre, barren, yet captivating scenery is just an hour-and-a-half from home.

You'll see canyons, coulees and hoodoos sculpted by the great masters: wind and water.

You'll see our naked, sensuous earth in every shade of brown: amber, brick, ochre, chocolate, copper, khaki, mahogany, tan, russet, terracotta, auburn, bronze, chestnut, ginger, henna, cinnamon, rust, cocoa, coffee, copper, and burnt sienna.

On the Dinosaur Trail

You'll see life-size dinosaur replicas on street corners. One of them, billed as the world's largest, towers above nearby buildings. Drumheller is, after all, home to the Royal Tyrrell Museum of Palaeontology.

You'll see oil wells bobbing ceaselessly in the grassland, themselves resembling artfully abstract dinosaurs.

You'll see the funky hamlet of Wayne, staving off ghost-townhood with admirable charm. En route you'll pass numerous homesteads—some quaint, others squalid, all intriguing to the passing voyeur.

And you'll see it all to best advantage—slowly and up close—from the seat of a bicycle, on smoothly paved highways where vehicle traffic is light enough to ignore.

Choose from two rides: a short, level, out-and-back trip through an intimate canyon to Wayne, or a long, hilly, panoramic loop around the valley.

Eroded walls of Drumheller Valley

Keen riders enjoy both in a single day. If riding with children, go to Wayne, but skip the busier Highway 10 section by starting in Rosedale instead of Drumheller.

fact

getting there

From Calgary, drive north on Highway 2. Just beyond Airdrie, turn right (east) onto Highway 72.

Pass through Beiseker. Continue east on Highway 9, eventually curving north into downtown Drumheller.

At the intersection with Highway 10, proceed straight across the railroad tracks onto 5th Street East. Follow it north toward the Red Deer River where it curves left past a dinosaur replica and becomes Riverside Drive East.

Immediately before reaching the Tourist Info Centre and a monumental dinosaur replica, turn right into Centennial Park.

Drive through the spacious lot and park next to the bike path. The elevation here is 670 m (2198 ft).

the rides

Wayne

From Centennial Park, ride east on the bike path, away from the Aquaplex and Tourist Info Centre.

Curve southeast behind the **baseball field**, following the Red Deer River downstream. At 0.7 km (0.4 mi), the path merges with the street.

Go left on **Riverside Drive East**. The path resumes at 1.4 km (0.9 mi), on the left, beneath cottonwoods and spruce trees. But it's easiest to stay on the broad street.

After curving right, behind the high-school athletic field, reach a stoplight at 2.7 km (1.7 mi). Turn left (southeast) onto **Highway 10**, also known as "the Hoodoo Trail."

At 7.5 km (4.7 mi) enter the village of Rosedale. At 8 km (5 mi) turn right (southwest) onto **Highway 10X**, known as the "Road of 11 Bridges."

One of 11 bridges en route to Wayne

Stegosaurus in downtown Drumheller

Pass the Rosedale Community Hall, then bear left to cross the first bridge at 8.4 km (5.2 mi). A pleasant campground in a cottonwood grove is just beyond, on the right.

The road is narrow, but cars are few and the canyon scenery is engaging. You're following **Rosebud Creek** upstream.

Beyond the ninth bridge spanning the creek, enter **Wayne** at 14 km (8.7 mi). A sign humbly acknowledges that the town's population used to be 2490 but is now only 42.

Turn right to visit the historic Rosedale Hotel and Last Chance Saloon. Or proceed straight to cross two more bridges and reach the end of pavement at 14.8 km (9.2 mi).

There are two campgrounds in Wayne: one near the hotel, the other between the last two bridges.

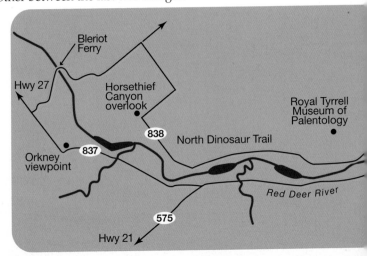

Dinosaur Trail Loop

From Centennial Park, ride west between the front of the Aquaplex (right) and the back of the Tourist Info Centre (left).

Pedal beneath the stupendous dinosaur replica. Pass the fountain, then turn right (northwest) onto the **bridge** spanning the Red Deer River.

You're now on Highway 9/56, but soon turn left (west) onto **Highway 838**. Known as "the Dinosaur Trail," it's signed for Midland Provincial Park.

Pass Midland Park at 4 km (2.5 mi) and the **Tyrrell Museum** at 6 km (3.7 mi). Enjoy level cycling for the first 45 minutes, gradually curving northwest.

The first steep ascent rewards you with an aerial view of the sheer-walled, multihued, Drumheller Valley. You're now cycling flat ground again atop a plateau, high above the river.

At 16 km (10 mi) a paved left fork descends to the **Horsethief Canyon viewpoint**. To continue on the Dinosaur Trail, bear right (east). Soon turn left (north) again.

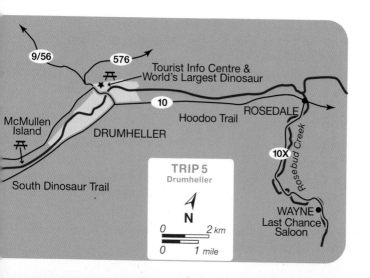

Crossing the Red Deer River on the Bleriot Ferry

At 21 km (13 mi), turn left (west). Ahead is a long, screaming downhill to the **Bleriot Ferry**. Don't ride your breaks. Let 'er rip. You won't fly into the river. The highway levels long before.

The ferry is named after Andre Bleriot, who homesteaded here in 1904. Bleriot's brother was the first person to fly across the English Channel.

Ironic, isn't it? Here you are, unable to fly, drive or even pedal yourself across the stone's-throw width of the shallow Red Deer River and therefore dependent on the services of a ferry whose namesake flew like a bird across a vast expanse of ocean.

The small, cable ferry operates daily, on-demand, 8 a.m. to 10:45 p.m. This is the loop's halfway point.

On the far bank, begin the second steep ascent: a long, granny-gear grind from the river to the plateau above the valley's west wall.

The climb ends at a T-junction across from a red barn. Go left (south) on **Highway 837**.

Secluded farm, Drumheller Valley

A few minutes farther, pass an unpaved left spur to **Orkney Lookout**. Continuing the Dinosaur Trail, a long, brisk descent ensues.

When it levels, the road parallels the river and affords frequent views of the languid, silty water and the riparian vegetation along its banks. Your general direction is now southeast.

Reach a T-junction at 46 km (28.6 mi). Go left. Gradually re-enter Drumheller through its industrial back door.

At the first stoplight, near the Husky gas station, go left (north) into downtown on **Highway 9**, which is 2nd Street West. The fountain and the colossal dinosaur where you began the ride are visible ahead.

Rapeseed (canola) near Drumheller Valley

trip 6
sheep river valley

route	paved Highway 546
location	30 minutes southwest of Calgary, in Kananaskis Country, west of Turner Valley
round trip	36 km (22.4 mi) from winter barricade 76 km (47.2 mi) from Turner Valley
elevation gain	300 m (984 ft) from barricade 645 m (2116 ft) from Turner Valley
cycling time	2 to 5 hours
difficulty	easy to moderate
map	Gem Trek *Bragg Creek and Sheep Valley, Kananaskis Country*

opinion

Global oil production, we've been told, has topped out.

Yet our demand for oil continues increasing while world supplies decline.

Something has to give. Apparently it will be our fossil-fuel-dependent economy.

Experts have described the apocalyptic future that awaits us when the price of gas rockets into the stratosphere causing modern society to wobble, stumble and collapse.

It's ugly, especially if you contemplate it while in your car, stuck in city traffic, during your daily commute.

But try looking at it from the seat of your bike, on a road where there are no cars. It's beautiful.

The place to sample the pedal-powered portion of a sustainable future is Highway 546, in the Sheep River Valley.

Sheep River Trail, late May

The time to do it is while the final 18 km (11.2 mi) are closed to motorists. The highway is open to all after May 14.

The closure protects wildlife that congregates in the valley during winter. In spring, the animals disperse when they can again feed in higher, more remote terrain.

Fit, keen cyclists should begin in the town of Turner Valley. Traffic is light from there on. If you're less ambitious, start at the barricade 20 km (12.4 mi) west of town.

Either way, you'll ride through rangeland and forested foothills toward the soaring peaks of the Great Divide. If you feel you're entering a movie scene, it's because you are. Countless Westerns have been filmed in this region.

By mid-May the pastures should be rapidly greening-up. Watch for deer and elk bounding across the highway. In the wetland ponds, you'll likely see geese feeding, preening and posturing, just like teenagers.

Sheep River Falls

The trip's scenic highlight is Sheep River Falls, 15 km (9.3 mi) past the highway barricade. The water tumbles over a graceful escarpment, explodes into a white maelstrom, then flows into a hypnotically serene, lapis-lazuli pool.

From Turner Valley to where the highway ends in 38 km (23.6 mi) at Junction Creek picnic area, ups and downs are minor with only one exception. But overall you'll ascend toward the mountains, which ensures a fast, easy, fun return.

Afterward, don't settle for the usual post-ride fare. Forget that brown banana and half-eaten Power Bar you left in the car. Instead, dine at the Route 40 Soup Company in Turner Valley (933-7676, www.route40sc.ca).

Here you can indulge in Lake Fish Crisp Wonton Ravioli with Green Tomato Tartar and Roasted Pepper Relish, or a plateful of Road Chips: seasoned blue, red, and Yukon Gold potatoes, served with an array of dips.

Now that's the way to celebrate that gasoline is still cheap enough that you can afford to drive out of the city to places like this, where cycling is safe, relaxing, and beautiful.

fact

getting there

From Calgary, drive generally southwest about 63 km (39 mi) to Turner Valley. If starting your ride there, park off Main Street at the Community Hall or Municipal Centre. If you want to cycle only the section of highway closed to motorists, continue driving west 20 km (12.4 mi) from the town centre.

the ride

Pedal south on Main Street to the stop sign. Turn right (west) onto **Sunset Boulevard**. The elevation here is 1080 m (3543 ft). A moderate ascent on this residential thoroughfare leads out of town.

Sheep River Trail, mid April

At 2.2 km (1.4 mi) the grade eases. A gentle descent ensues. You're now on **Highway 546**. It's broad, smoothly paved, with a shoulder affording cyclists a margin of safety.

The Front Range of the Rockies leaps into view at 3 km (1.9 mi). The peaks are still impressively snow-laden in mid-May.

Settle into a cadence at 4.6 km (2.9 mi) where the highway levels before undulating through rangeland and forested foothills.

Enter **Kananaskis Country** at 15.3 km (9.5 mi). The highway deteriorates here. Though paved, it's cracked, potholed, crudely patched, and has no marked shoulder.

After piercing a ravine, the highway is even rougher for about a kilometer. The dusting of gravel on the asphalt will make road bikers grimace, but the surface is passable on skinny tires.

The highway improves at 18.5 km (11.5 mi), near the Sheep River Parks office. At 20 km (12.4 mi) proceed west through a junction, pass a public phone on the right, and arrive at the **winter barricade**. The elevation here is 1425 m (4675 ft).

It's still closed? Lucky you. Dismount, hoist your bike over, and pedal on. The quality of the highway varies ahead but it remains paved.

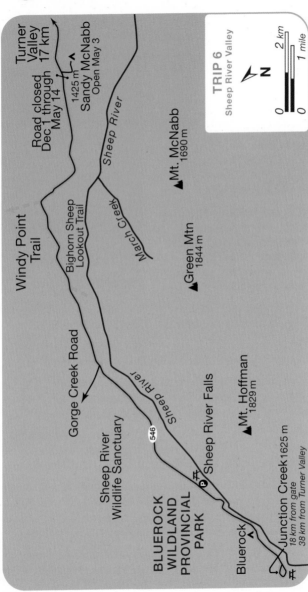

TRIP 6
Sheep River Valley

N

0   2 km
0   1 mile

Turner
Valley
17 km

Road closed
Dec 1 through
May 14

1425 m

Sandy McNabb
Open May 3

Windy Point
Trail

Bighorn Sheep
Lookout Trail

Sheep River

▲Mt. McNabb
1690 m

March Creek

Gorge Creek Road

▲Green Mtn
1844 m

Sheep River
Wildlife Sanctuary

546

Sheep River

Sheep River Falls

P

▲Mt. Hoffman
1829 m

BLUEROCK
WILDLAND
PROVINCIAL
PARK

Bluerock

Junction Creek 1625 m
18 km from gate
38 km from Turner Valley

Sheep River Trail descending into Gorge Creek

What continues improving is the scenery. The Front Range looms ever higher. The Sheep River is below you in a deep canyon.

Ups and downs are minor until you pass **Gorge Creek** Trail, a dirt road forking right at 29 km (18 mi). Here you plummet for a couple exhilarating minutes, then pay for it by grinding up a long, steep hill.

Beyond, the highway again poses no difficulties. At 35 km (21.7 mi) turn left into **Sheep River Falls picnic area**. Walk 130 m (142 yd) downstream to a bench overlooking the falls.

If you cycle the highway past the falls, you'll be rewarded with a brief stretch where the pavement is next to the river.

At 38 km (23.6 mi), the highway ends with a flourish by looping through **Junction Creek picnic area**. The elevation here is 1625 m (5331 ft).

Both Sheep River Falls and Junction Creek picnic areas have riverside tables where you can rest and enjoy lunch before heading home.

trip 7
highwood pass

route	paved Highway 40
location	45 minutes southwest of Calgary, in Kananaskis Country
round trip	34 km (21 mi) to Highwood Pass 108 km (67 mi) to Highwood Junction
elevation gain	536 to 1267 m (1758 to 4157 ft)
cycling time	2 to 5 hours
difficulty	moderate to challenging
map	Gem Trek *Kananaskis Lakes*

opinion

Racers wearing peacockish, logo-crazy cycling jerseys were there, checking their heart-rate monitors while hammering sculpted, carbon-fibre road machines.

Parents towing tots on trailercycles were there, climbing the hills like yaks, straining under the burden yet smiling beatifically.

A 70-year-old couple was there, pedaling warhorse touring bikes, training for their ride across Croatia later this summer.

Kids on squeaking, screw-loose, derelict mountain bikes were there, unzipped hoodies ballooning in the breeze, helmets bouncing on their heads like dashboard doggies.

It was a typical spring weekend on Highway 40 in Kananaskis Country.

The pavement was free of snow. The winter gates were closed, keeping it free of motorists. And dozens of Calgarians were enjoying what has become an annual street fair for cyclists—unofficial but wildly popular.

Mt. Kidd, above Highway 40

Heading southeast toward Highwood Pass

Any road closure granting dominion to cyclists is cause for celebration, but this one is special.

It's long: 54 km (33.6 mi) from the north gate at King Creek to the south gate at Highwood Junction.

It's lofty. Topping out nearly in the alpine zone at 2206-m (7238-ft) Highwood Pass, this is the highest public road in Canada.

It's spectacular, traversing a mountain vastness enshrined within provincial parklands.

The price of admission, however, is steep. The gentle ascent from King Creek slowly builds to a granny-gear chore.

If this were the Tour de France route, the length and grade of the final skyward climb to the pass would earn it a Category 1 rating. The scale ranges from 4 (least challenging) to 1 (most challenging). Only a few pivotal, excruciating climbs earn a rating of "beyond category."

Moderately strong riders will crest the pass within 1¼ hours. If you're slower, you'll simply get to enjoy the scenery longer—a good thing, because on the way back you'll coast far enough and fast enough to make your eyes water.

Highway 40, early June

Feeling sapped, eager to claim their downhill reward, most people turn around at the pass. Lay off the brakes and you'll arrive at King Creek in about 45 minutes.

But if you have more time and can endure another ascent similar to the one you just completed, pedal through the pass and swoop into the Highwood River Valley.

Here's where the atmosphere changes from street fair to backcountry adventure, because you'll see few other cyclists. It's like trail riding, only speedier, smoother, easier.

The gate near Highwood Junction is about an hour beyond the pass for moderately strong riders. But near where the highway levels and your coasting velocity slows, several picnic areas will tempt you to abort the journey and rest before climbing back to the pass.

The scenery remains engaging the entire way, and of course your sense of accomplishment increases the farther you go. But the best reason to tag the south gate is simply to take full advantage of the highway closure.

The gates close December 1. They reopen and vehicle traffic resumes June 16. But Highwood Pass usually isn't snow-free until late May. By November, traversing it might require snowshoes.

So you have perhaps three weeks. That's not a window of opportunity. It's a peephole. Don't miss it.

fact

getting there

From Calgary, drive Highway 1 west. Take the Highway 40 exit and continue south 50 km (31 mi) into Kananaskis Country.

Slow down at King Creek Day Use Area (left). Shortly beyond, Kananaskis Lakes Trail (right) departs Highway 40. Just past that intersection is the winter gate halting motorists December 1 through June 15.

The elevation here is 1670 m (5479 ft). Park at King Creek, or beside the highway if the gate is closed.

the ride

From the **north gate** near King Creek, begin a gentle ascent south on Highway 40 beneath Mt. Wintour (left).

After a short descent, a moderate climb leads to where **Valley View Trail** (a dirt road) forks left. Proceed south on the highway.

Over your right shoulder (northwest) the Spray Mountains and Kananaskis Range are impressive. Right (west) are the enormous peaks ringing Upper Kananaskis Lake.

Within 45 minutes, you'll be next to **Pocaterra Creek**. Pass a gated dirt road forking right. Attention mountain bikers: it leads to Elk Lakes Provincial Park. The highway curves left (east) here.

Ignore **Little Highwood Pass Day Use Area**. It's just a tiny parking lot without picnic tables. The ascent soon begins in earnest. You have five relentlessly uphill kilometers to go.

Though Elpoca Mountain (left / north) is an extraordinary sight, it's difficult to appreciate while attempting to defy gravity.

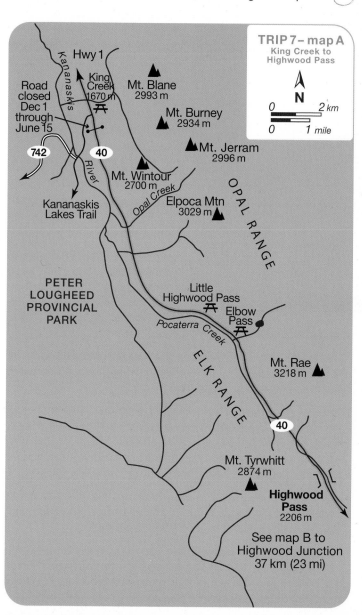

TRIP 7 – map A
King Creek to
Highwood Pass

N

0 — 2 km
0 — 1 mile

Hwy 1

Kananaskis

Road closed Dec 1 through June 15

742

40

King Creek 1670 m

Mt. Blane 2993 m

Mt. Burney 2934 m

Mt. Jerram 2996 m

Mt. Wintour 2700 m

Kananaskis River

Opal Creek

Kananaskis Lakes Trail

Elpoca Mtn 3029 m

OPAL RANGE

PETER LOUGHEED PROVINCIAL PARK

Little Highwood Pass

Elbow Pass

Pocaterra Creek

ELK RANGE

Mt. Rae 3218 m

40

Mt. Tyrwhitt 2874 m

Highwood Pass 2206 m

See map B to Highwood Junction 37 km (23 mi)

Opal Falls, from Highway 40

Should you need a rest, **Elbow Pass Day Use Area** is just ahead and does have a couple tables.

Heading southwest now, the highway climbs between Mt. Rae (left) and Pocaterra Ridge (right). The ridgecrest trail is a rewarding hike in summer.

Reach 2206-m (7238-ft) **Highwood Pass** at 17 km (10.6 mi). Before turning around, pedal far enough to see the highway plunge into the forest beyond.

Keen cyclists will take that plunge, rocketing southeast into the Highwood River Valley, cruising past **Mt. Lipsett Recreation Area** at 23.2 km (14.4 mi), and curving east beneath Mist Mountain (left).

The downhill thrill is over near **Mist Creek Recreation Area** at 34.5 km (21.4 mi). You're not aiming for Highwood Junction? Relax here beside the Highwood River.

Resuming southeast, Picklejar, Trout Ponds, Lantern Creek, and Lineham Creek recreation areas are at 35, 35.7, 37.6, and 43 km (21.7, 22.2, 23.4, and 26.7 mi). The others, at Cat and Fitzsimmons creeks, are close enough to Highwood Junction that you might as well fluff your pride by finishing the task.

Reach the **south gate** at 54 km (33.6 mi), 1475 m (4839 ft). Immediately beyond is **Highwood Junction**, where Highway 541 proceeds east, and Highway 940 turns south.

The junction's sole enterprise is the Highwood House store, which opens each year on May 1. So before starting the two-hour ride back to the pass, you can do more than refill water bottles. You can indulge your Homer Simpson-size craving for snacks.

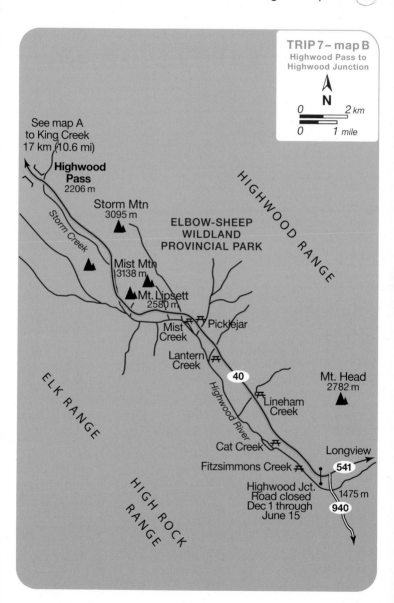

TRIP 7 – map B
Highwood Pass to
Highwood Junction

N

0   2 km
0   1 mile

See map A
to King Creek
17 km (10.6 mi)

**Highwood
Pass**
2206 m

Storm Creek

Storm Mtn
3095 m

HIGHWOOD RANGE

ELBOW-SHEEP
WILDLAND
PROVINCIAL PARK

Mist Mtn
3138 m

Mt. Lipsett
2580 m

Picklejar

Mist
Creek

Lantern
Creek

40

Highwood River

Mt. Head
2782 m

Lineham
Creek

ELK RANGE

Cat Creek

Longview

Fitzsimmons Creek

541

Highwood Jct.
Road closed
Dec 1 through
June 15

1475 m

940

HIGH ROCK
RANGE

trip 8
bow valley parkway

route	paved Highway 1A
location	1½ hours west of Calgary, in Banff National Park, between Banff townsite and Lake Louise Village
round trip	99 km (61.5 mi), with shorter options
elevation gain	360 m (1181 ft), less for shorter options
cycling time	4 hours, with shorter options
difficulty	easy to moderate
map	Gem Trek *Banff & Mount Assiniboine*

opinion

Sensational scenery is high-octane fuel. You fill up with your eyes and your heart pumps it to your muscles.

So you should experience no shortage of energy while cycling Highway 1A—the Bow Valley Parkway—from near Banff townsite to Lake Louise Village.

This ribbon of pavement following the Bow River in Banff National Park is lined with soaring mountains: the Sawback Range, the Massive Range, the Panorama Range.

Every upward glance is like a sip of PowerBar Gel, because your stamina is affected by your attitude, and your attitude is boosted by exhilarating sights.

The culminating view is of glacier-hatted Mt. Temple and the ice-encrusted peaks ringing Lake Louise. You'll see them before cruising into the village.

That's when your attention will likely shift from inspirational fuel to the kind you can stuff into your mouth, which is why most cyclists wheel directly into the Samson Mall and line up for fresh goodies at Laggan's Mountain Bakery and Deli (522-2017).

Mt. Ishbel, Bow Valley Parkway

Heading southwest on Bow Valley Parkway

Though the highway parallels the frenetic Trans-Canada, it's distinctly separate and substantially less busy. Cyclists find it serene and safe until RV traffic picks up in summer. It lacks a painted shoulder-line, but it's comfortably broad, and most people who drive it aren't in a rush.

No reason for cyclists to rush either. If moderately strong, you can ride the full round trip in about four hours, leaving you ample time to rest and rubberneck at the many picnic areas, viewpoint pullouts, and campgrounds en route.

At Johnston Canyon you can lock your steed to a tree, waddle up the path, and see a lusty creek cascade into a deep, dark, cool, narrow chasm. Less ambitious cyclists turn around here, just shy of half way.

That first half of the ride is the hilliest. North of Castle Mountain Village, the highway remains relatively level for about 10 km (6.2 mi). Nowhere will you face a withering ascent. The ups are just steep enough to ensure you enjoy coasting down the other side.

Model T at Johnston Canyon Resort

Granted, Highway 1A isn't entirely smooth. Enough cracks span the pavement that you might wonder if this is the original Bow Valley road constructed in the early 1900s. It's annoying—ker-thunk, ker-thunk—especially on a sexy, slender-tired velocipede designed for speed rather than commotion.

But the bumps are small and the scenery is huge. Cyclists have every reason to grin while pedaling this world-class bike route.

fact

before your trip

To see the Banff National Park entry-fee schedule prior to arriving at the park gate, visit www.pc.gc.ca/pn-np/ab/banff, click on "visitor information," then click on "fees."

getting there

Drive Highway 1 west into Banff National Park. Just 5.5 km (3.4 mi) past the second Banff townsite interchange, exit onto Highway 1A, also called the Bow Valley Parkway.

At 5.8 km (3.6 mi) bear right. At 6 km (3.7 mi) turn right at the sign for Fireside picnic area. There's room for a couple vehicles to park at the beginning of this access road, just off the pavement, at 1410 m (4626 ft).

You'll find more parking 2 km (1.2 mi) farther west, on the left (south) side of the Parkway.

the ride

Heading west, the pavement is fairly level. You can pedal at an easy warm-up pace while nestling into that sweet spot on your saddle.

The highway soon splits, allowing only one-way traffic. The lanes rejoin shortly beyond. This happens twice more ahead, but for longer stretches, granting you more time to enjoy reduced vehicle traffic.

After the highway unites beyond the first split, it curves north-west. This will remain your general direction of travel all the way to Lake Louise Village.

Past **Muleshoe picnic area**, you'll notice charred trees—the result of a prescribed burn in 1993. The next generation forest is still only a meter tall. But within fifteen minutes you'll spurt back into untorched woodland of primarily fir, aspen, and lodgepole pine.

After Sawback picnic area, enter scenic **Hillsdale Meadows** at 12 km (7.5 mi). The panorama comprises 2931-m (9616-ft) Mt. Bourgeau to the south, and 2908-m (9541-ft) Mt. Ishbel to the north.

The Post Hotel at Lake Louise Village

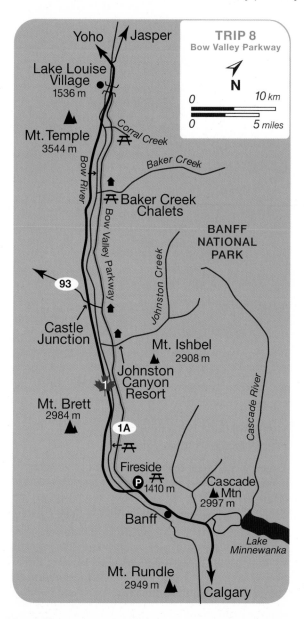

TRIP 8
Bow Valley Parkway

N

0   10 km

0   5 miles

Yoho   Jasper

Lake Louise
Village
1536 m

Corral Creek

Baker Creek

Mt. Temple
3544 m

Baker Creek
Chalets

BANFF
NATIONAL
PARK

Bow River

Bow Valley Parkway

Johnston Creek

93

Castle
Junction

Mt. Ishbel
2908 m

Johnston
Canyon
Resort

Cascade River

Mt. Brett
2984 m

1A

Fireside
P 1410 m

Cascade
Mtn
2997 m

Banff

Lake
Minnewanka

Mt. Rundle
2949 m

Calgary

Castle Mountain, from Johnston Canyon Resort

Reach **Johnston Canyon** at 17 km (10.6 mi). It's an easy ten-minute walk to the lower falls concealed within the bowels of this impressive rift. It's hardly any walk at all into the rustic resort, where ice cream is concealed behind the counter.

Castle Mountain Village, at 23 km (14.3 mi), has a small grocery store and nine picnic tables beneath fantastically complex Castle Mountain. A left turn here leads southwest to Highways 1 and 93 at nearby Castle Junction. Proceed northwest on Highway 1A.

A viewpoint pullout at 25.2 km (15.7 mi) invites you to gaze at 3161-m (10,371-ft) Storm Mountain, southwest across the valley. At 33 km (20.5 mi) begin a long, level stretch. Pass the **Baker Creek Chalets** at 37.2 km (23.1 mi).

Glimpse Mt. Temple left (west) at 41.8 km (26 mi). From this humbling perspective, it's hard to believe droves of hikers, armed with nothing more technical than trekking poles, reach the summit every summer. The task at hand is small in comparison. Pedal on. Your goal is within reach.

Corral Creek picnic area, at 45.7 km (28.4 mi), is a more tranquil place to rest and eat than Lake Louise Village offers. If you don't stop here prior to visiting the village, do so on the way back—with your jersey pockets full of treats from Laggan's Bakery.

At 48.5 km (30.1 mi) arrive at a T-junction. Left descends west to **Lake Louise Village**, within view, at 49.5 km (30.8 mi). Gliding into the village, you'll see the mountains ringing the actual *Lake* Louise—a spectacle worthy of today's most overused and undervalued adjective: awesome.

trip 9

waterton lakes national park

route	paved Akamina and Red Rock parkways
location	3 hours south of Calgary
round trip	32 to 66 km (20 to 41 mi)
elevation gain	215 to 595 m (705 to 1952 ft)
cycling time	2 to 4¼ hours
difficulty	moderate
map	Gem Trek *Waterton Lakes National Park*

opinion

Waterton Lakes National Park is a UNESCO World Heritage Site, an International Peace Park, and a Biosphere Reserve.

It's the only park on the planet with all three designations.

It's also downright beautiful. Peaks, lakes, forests, meadows, everything you'd expect of the Canadian Rockies is here, spiced by the prevalence of argillite, a rock that gives much of the landscape an exotic red or green hue.

Yet Waterton is small, eclipsed by larger, more famous parks: U.S. Glacier National Park immediately south, Banff National Park farther north.

It's not on a major highway. It's not even convenient once you're there. You can drive into it, but not through it. You have to turn around and exit the way you came.

So relatively few people poke their noses into Waterton Park.

Of those, some never dislodge themselves from their automobiles. They pop in, peer up at the mountains through the windshield, say "Wow!" then depart, all in about an hour.

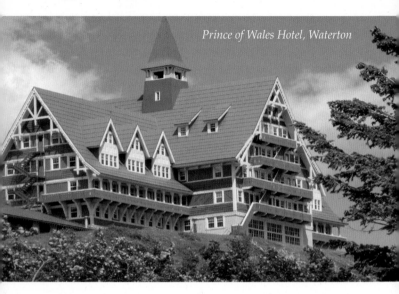

Prince of Wales Hotel, Waterton

A smattering come to pitch their tent or park their RV—enough to fill up the two campgrounds in summer. A portion of those go hiking. Almost none go biking beyond the tiny townsite.

On a couple occasions, we've been the only cyclists in the entire park. Yet Waterton offers road riding as easy and scenic as any in Alberta.

Starting at a shady picnic area beside Upper Waterton Lake, you have a choice of two routes. Ideally, ride one in the morning, return for a lazy, lakeside lunch, then ride the other. Each is distinctly different.

Akamina Parkway to Cameron Lake

A demanding ascent soon relaxes into a gradual, rolling climb. Below you is Cameron Creek canyon. The rambunctious creek will be your occasional escort.

You'll probe a narrow, treed valley. After pedaling 16 km (10 mi) and gaining 380 m (1247 ft) in about 1¼ hours, you'll reach Cameron Lake at 1660 m (5446 ft) in a stupendous cirque.

Vimy Peak above Waterton townsite, from Akamina Parkway

You'll have to pedal only briefly on the way back. The final descent is especially swift. Upon reaching Upper Waterton Lake in about 45 minutes, your total distance will be 32 km (20 mi).

Red Rock Parkway to Red Rock Canyon

The parkway begins with a sharp ascent, then undulates erratically before settling into a moderate climb into broad Blakiston Creek valley.

You'll pedal through rolling grassland where wildflowers bloom May through July. The expansive view comprises soft, verdant ridges and austere crags.

Mt. Blakiston dominates the skyline up-valley, where you'll reach the road's end parking lot at 17 km (10.6 mi), 1495 m (4905 ft) having gained 215 m (705 ft) in about 1½ hours. Red Rock Creek flows out of Red Rock Canyon here.

The gravity-powered return trip is fast. It's possible to zip back within 45 minutes. In this direction, Mt. Vimy is a compelling sight. Upon reaching Upper Waterton Lake, your total distance will be 34 km (21.1 mi).

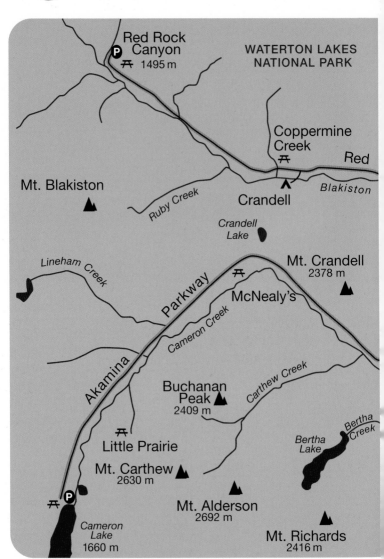

Red Rock
Canyon
1495 m

WATERTON LAKES
NATIONAL PARK

Coppermine
Creek
Red

Mt. Blakiston

Ruby Creek

Blakiston

Crandell

Crandell
Lake

Lineham Creek

Parkway

Mt. Crandell
2378 m

McNealy's

Cameron Creek

Akamina

Carthew Creek

Buchanan
Peak
2409 m

Bertha
Creek

Bertha
Lake

Little Prairie

Mt. Carthew
2630 m

Mt. Alderson
2692 m

Cameron
Lake
1660 m

Mt. Richards
2416 m

Red Rock Canyon

Buffalo Paddock

Lethbridge

6

Rock Parkway

Creek

Lower Waterton Lake

5

Pass Creek ⛺

Sofa Creek

Prince of Wales Hotel

Driftwood ⛺ Beach

Middle Waterton Lake

⛺

⛺ Waterton town 1280 m

Vimy Peak ▲ 2379 m

Upper Waterton Lake

TRIP 9
Waterton Lakes National Park

↑ N

0 — 2 km
0 — 1 mile

High mountains surround you on Akamina Parkway.

Both parkways are narrow and lack designated shoulders, but motorists tend to drive slowly and carefully here. They're on vacation, so they have time to be courteous to cyclists.

If you must choose just one of the two rides, consult the notorious Waterton wind.

It's blowing hard? Opt for Akamina Parkway, where the narrow valley will shelter you. The price of protection is restricted views, but the Cameron Lake cirque at road's will compensate.

It's calm? You're lucky. Ride the Red Rock Parkway, where you'll enjoy constant views but would be severely battered by a gale.

fact

before your trip

To see the Waterton National Park entry-fee schedule prior to arriving at the park gate, visit www.pc.gc.ca/pn-np/ab/waterton, click on "visitor information," then click on "fees."

getting there

From Calgary, drive Highway 2 south to Fort MacLeod, Highway 3 southwest to Pincher Creek, then Highway 6 south to Waterton Lakes National Park.

From the entry gate continue southwest 7.6 km (4.7 mi), then turn left into an unnamed picnic area beside Upper Waterton Lake.

This picnic area is 300 m (328 yd) south of the Info Centre, immediately below the Prince of Wales Hotel, directly across from Akamina Parkway, and just before Waterton townsite. The elevation here is 1280 m (4200 ft).

the rides

Akamina Parkway

From the picnic area, cross the main road, and proceed onto the parkway. Begin a steep climb southwest. The grade eases in about 20 minutes, heading northwest.

Attain views over Waterton townsite, across Upper Waterton Lake to Vimy Peak, and into Cameron Creek canyon. The surrounding forest is a mix of pine and aspen.

Pass **McNealy's picnic area**, beside Cameron Creek, at 6.5 km (4 mi). It has a shelter and toilets. The road curves southwest here.

Pass the site of **western Canada's first oil well** at 8.5 km (5.3 mi). It was drilled in 1901. Left (southeast) across the creek is 2623-m (8606-ft) Mt. Carthew.

The Lineham Creek and Rowe Lakes trailheads are at 9.3 and 10.5 km (5.8 and 6.5 mi). Forum Peak, which rises above Cameron Lake, is visible ahead (southwest). The **Akamina Pass trailhead** is at 14.6 km (9.1 mi).

After turning south, the road ends at 16 km (10 mi), 1660 m (5446 ft), near the north shore of **Cameron Lake**. There's a picnic area here. Beyond the south shore is 2708-m (8885-ft) Mt. Custer.

Red Rock Parkway

From the picnic area, return to the main road, turn right and follow it north past the **info centre**.

In 3 km (1.9 mi), cross the **Blakiston Creek bridge**, turn left onto the parkway, and follow it generally north-northwest. After a couple stiff climbs and speedy descents, the road ascends gently through rolling fescue grassland.

*Unnamed peak above
Akamina Parkway*

Wildflowers flourish here. You might see purple lupine, fuchsia herb-willow, yellow balsamroot, pink plumed avens, cobalt larkspur, yellow asters, or amber brown-eyed susans.

Curve west to enter **Blakiston Creek valley** at 9.5 km (5.9 mi). Left (south) is 2378-m (7802-ft) Mt. Crandell. Descend past Crandell Campground at 9.8 km (5.9 mi), then resume ascending.

Pass **Coppermine Creek picnic area** at 11 km (6.8 mi). It has a shelter and toilets. Ahead (west) is 2940-m (9656-ft) Mt. Blakiston.

A long descent levels at 13.6 km (8.5 mi). **Lost Horse Creek picnic** area is at 14.7 km (9.1 mi). It has a shelter and toilets.

At 17 km (10.6 mi), 1495 m (4905 ft), the road ends at Red Rock Creek, beneath **Red Rock Canyon**. Just 300 m (328 yd) back is a quiet, creekside picnic area.

trip 10
icefields parkway (promenade des glaciers)

route	paved Highway 93
location	2¼ hours northwest of Calgary, in Banff National Park, northwest of Lake Louise Village
round trip	74 km (46 mi) to Bow Summit
	146 km (90.5 mi) to Saskatchewan Crossing
elevation gain	479 m (1571 ft) to Bow Summit
	1103 m (3619 ft) to Saskatchewan Crossing
cycling time	4 to 8 hours
difficulty	moderate to challenging
maps	Gem Trek *Lake Louise & Yoho* and/or *Bow Lake and Saskatchewan Crossing* Or visit www.pc.gc.ca/pn-np/ab/jasper visit/visit38_E.asp for a free Parks Canada download.

opinion

"This wondertrail will be world renowned," a surveyor predicted.

It was 1920. He was looking north into a vast, untracked, wilderness valley girded by looming peaks, 600 glaciers, and six icefields.

Construction began in the early 1930s, thanks to a public-works unemployment-relief program. In 1940 the Icefields Parkway opened, stretching 230 km (143 mi) from Lake Louise Village to the town of Jasper.

Bow Lake and Crowfoot Glacier

Wondertrail indeed. Some went so far as to call it "50 Switzer-lands in one." And for mechanical-horse jockeys, it's especially wondrous. Because this isn't a mere trail, or even a four-wheel-drive road. It's a paved highway.

Google the phrase "most spectacular highway" and you'll discover it's a cliché carelessly ascribed to various ribbons of pavement from Florida to Alaska.

But the parkway consistently ranks among the top search results. If cyclists voted, it would be permanently enshrined at the top of the heap.

The majority of those who've ridden it in good weather will tell you: No paved road in North America rivals the parkway for sheer spectacle wattage.

That's why bicycle-tour companies from across the continent bring big-spending clients to ride the entire parkway in three

Herbert Lake and, from left to right,
Mounts Temple, St. Piran, Niblock and Whyte

or four days. You, however, can ride a substantial chunk of it in a single day and pay nothing for the privilege.

Though the parkway parallels the Great Divide, backbone of the continent, it's well engineered, so the grade is never steep. The only structural drawback is cracked pavement caused by deeply frigid winter temperatures, which prevents you from enjoying a smooth ride.

Transport trucks are barred from the parkway, and the shoulder is generous most of the way, but it has only two-lanes, and summer tourist traffic—RVs as well as cars—is substantial. Between late June and mid-September, 1,150 vehicles travel the parkway each day.

That's why the ideal times to cycle it are mid-May through mid-June, and mid-September through mid-October. With fewer vehicles whooshing past, you can relax, marvel at the scenery, and watch for wildlife.

Mt. Wilson, above Saskatchewan Crossing

While pedaling the parkway, you might see elk, moose, mountain goats, black bears, or grizzly bears. We've seen them all within the span of a few hours.

Starting just north of Lake Louise, strong cyclists undertake a 146-km (90.5-mi) round trip to Saskatchewan Crossing, where fur trappers forded the North Saskatchewan River en route to British Columbia in the 1800s. Today you'll find a resort there, including a restaurant where you can tank-up for the return ride.

If Saskatchewan Crossing is beyond your range, shorten the endeavour to a 74-km (46-mi) round trip by stopping at Bow Summit—the scenic climax and highpoint on this stretch of the parkway.

By turning around there, you'll spare yourself having to attain the summit twice. Still, your day in the saddle will likely be among your life's most memorable.

fact

before your trip

To see the Banff National Park entry-fee schedule prior to arriving at the park gate, visit www.pc.gc.ca/pn-np/ab/banff, click on "visitor information," then click on "fees."

getting there

From Calgary, drive Hwy 1 west. Pass Canmore, enter Banff National Park, and continue beyond Banff townsite to Lake Louise. But don't exit there. Proceed another 2 km (1.2 mi) northwest, then bear right onto Highway 93—the Icefields Parkway. About 3.5 km (2.2 mi) farther, turn left (west) into the Herbert Lake picnic area, at 1590 m (5215 ft). Mt. Temple is visible southeast.

the ride

There are no junctions on this stretch of the parkway, so you really don't need directions. Saddle up, pedal northwest as far as fitness, curiosity and daylight allow, then turn around. It's that simple.

But anticipation and pride are a potent brew. Looking forward to what's ahead, and knowing how much progress you've made, can fuel your forward motion. So referring to the route description below should help you cycle farther and enjoy the trip more than you otherwise might.

1 km (0.6 mi)
Begin a gradual ascent.

15 km (9.3 mi)
Hector Lake overlook is on the left. At the foot of the Waputik Range, this 5.8-km (3.6-mi) lake is the second largest in Banff National Park.

20.5 km (12.7 mi)
Mosquito Creek campground is on the left. The picnic tables beside the Bow River are a tranquil spot for a rest break.

29.5 km (18.3 mi)
Having curved around Bow Peak's north side, **Crowfoot Glacier** is visible left. The glacier used to have three spurs resembling a crow's foot.

30.5 km (19 mi)
Bow Lake picnic area is on the left, near the lake's southeast end, beneath is 3050-m (10,006-ft) Crowfoot Mountain.

32.5 km (20.2 mi)
A gravel spur forks left to **Num-Ti-Jah Lodge**, on the northwest shore of Bow Lake. The rustic, red-roofed hotel you see today is the successor to a cabin built in 1923 by Jimmy Simpson, a legendary trapper and guide. At age 19, Simpson left England, came to the Rockies, and explored the Bow Valley while it was roadless.

37 km (23 mi)
After ascending through subalpine meadows, crest 2069-m (6788-ft) **Bow Summit**, which divides the watersheds of the

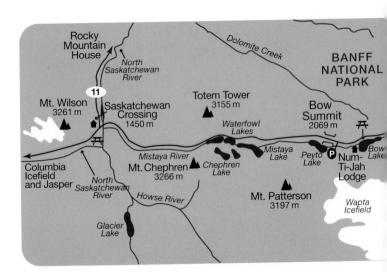

Bow and Mistaya Rivers. A paved spur forks left here, ascending 0.5 km (0.3 mi) to the **Peyto Lake** parking lot. From there, a paved footpath leads 0.4 km (0.25 mi) to a spectacular overlook at 2120 m (6955 ft), where you'll see the lake 260 m (853 ft) below. Suspended glacial rock-flour gives the lake its startling, opaque, turquoise colour.

Decision time

If you turn around at Bow Summit, your round-trip distance will be 74 km (46 mi) with an elevation gain of 479 m (1571 ft).

If you descend northwest and continue 36 km (22.3 mi) to Saskatchewan Crossing, you'll lose 624 m (2047 ft). You'll regain it on the return, while completing a 146-km (90.5-mi) round trip with a total elevation gain of 1103 m (3619 ft).

Continuing

Lose 354 m (1161 ft) on the 7-km (4.5-mi) descent into the Mistaya River Valley. The parkway levels at 1715 m (5627 ft), above the south end of Mistaya Lake.

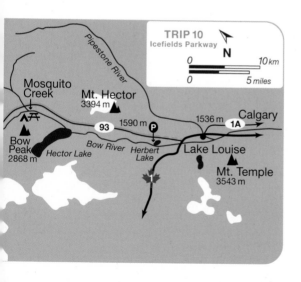

After that, the downhill grade is largely imperceptible until the final drop to Saskatchewan Crossing. What you might notice, however, is a warmer temperature in the lower-elevation, mixed-forest, montane zone.

54 km (33.5 mi)
Waterfowl Lakes campground is on the left, beneath 3266-m (10,715-ft) Mt. Chephren.

67.7 km (42 mi)
Between Mt. Sarbach (left / southwest) and Mt. Murchison (right / east) is a pullout on the left. From there, a trail descends about 12 minutes to a bridge over the **Mistaya River** where it surges through a deep, narrow, sensuously eroded cleft.

Mt. Chephren above Waterfowl Lake

72 km (44.6 mi)
Cross a bridge spanning the **North Saskatchewan River** at 1400 m (4593 ft). Its source is the Saskatchewan Glacier in the Columbia Icefield. During its 1,287-km (800-mi) course, the river flows through downtown Edmonton, eventually joins the Saskatchewan River, and finally empties into Lake Winnipeg, in Manitoba. Early travelers had trouble crossing the braided channels. Even in the 1930s, it was a challenge for highway engineers to construct the bridge now conveying you to the northwest bank.

73 km (45.3 mi)
Just past the Howse River Viewpoint picnic area on the left, the David Thompson Highway (11) forks right. Immediately beyond is **The Crossing Resort** (gas station, gift shop, restaurant, motel) at 1450 m (4757 ft). It's above the confluence of the Mistaya, North Saskatchewan, and Howse rivers, at the foot of 3261-m (10,700-ft) Mt. Wilson.

LE PELOTON

The Elbow Valley Cycle Club has been promoting cycling, and introducing cyclists to each other, since 1983. It now has about 1,000 members.

The club organizes rides and multi-day tours. It sponsors cycling skills programs. It works with city planners to develop bike-friendly policies and facilities in and around Calgary.

Calgarians appreciate the club for being a vital force behind their city's laudable effort to accommodate cyclists:

• Bicycles are allowed on the C-Train (Calgary's light-rail transit system) during off-peak hours.

• Calgary buses that stop at recreation areas are fitted with bike racks.

• A bike path links Calgary International Airport with the city pathway system, and there's a place at the airport where cyclists can assemble or disassemble their bikes.

• Calgary's major pathways are regularly cleared of snow.

Visit www.elbowvalleycc.org to learn about events you might enjoy, projects needing your volunteer support, and issues affecting you and your fellow cyclists.

PEDAL POWER

Bike Calgary is a local bike-commuter advocacy group. It informs, educates and inspires Calgary cyclists. It seeks to improve cycling-related city infrastructure and increase public respect for bicycles as transportation. Visit www.bikecalgary. org for advice on cycle commuting routes, and to learn about current cycling advocacy initiatives.

Canmore Nordic Centre

INFORMATION SOURCES

**Calgary Convention
and Visitors Bureau**
(800) 661-1678
www.tourismcalgary.com

Calgary Events Calendar
www.downtowncalgary.com

Calgary Pathway & Bikeways Map
www.elbowvalleycc.org
(see Links page to download the pdf)

City of Calgary
(403) 268-2489
www.calgary.ca

Weather
www.theweathernetwork.com

INDEX

THE AUTHORS

Their second date was a 32-km (20-mi) dayhike in Arizona. Eight months later, on a 75-km (47-mi) bike ride through the desert, Kathy and Craig committed to their journey together.

Hiking and cycling continued to define their relationship, propelling them toward a life of shared adventure and ultimately into a career of writing and publishing guidebooks.

Today they live in Canmore, Alberta, where they consider the long, frigid winters "writing season" and eagerly await spring—"riding season"—when they can get back on their road bikes.

"Cycling is a joy in itself," Kathy says, "but it's also a great way to train for summer hiking, and an exhilarating way to travel. On a bike, you don't just see the world, you experience it with all your senses, you get to know it viscerally."

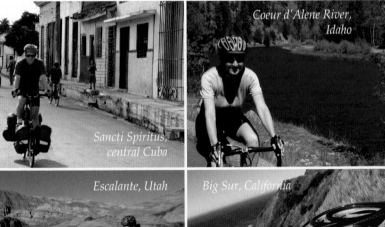

Coeur d'Alene River, Idaho

Sancti Spiritus, central Cuba

Escalante, Utah

Big Sur, California

Kathy and Craig have cycled the glass-smooth backroads of Provence, the potholed asphalt of Cuba, the utopian bikepaths of Holland, the tranquil byways of Oregon's Willamette Valley, the California Big Sur coast, Australia's Great Ocean Road, Utah's other-worldly canyon country, the lakeside highways of British Columbia and Washington, and the Trail of the Coeur d'Alenes—116 km (72 mi) of cycling paradise in the Idaho Panhandle (www.friendsofcdatrails.org).

To read an account of Kathy and Craig's cycling trip through Cuba, originally published as a travel feature in the Calgary Herald, visit hikingcamping.com. Click on "Guidebooks," "Cycling," and "Cycle Touring Cuba."

To post a description of a ride you've enjoyed and want to recommend to other keen cyclists, click on "Other Adventures," "On The Ground," and "Free Cycling-Trip Info."

Provence, France

Silver Valley, Idaho

Snow Canyon, Utah

Other Titles from hikingcamping.com

The following titles—boot-tested and written by the Opinionated Hikers, Kathy & Craig Copeland—are widely available in outdoor shops and bookstores. Visit www.hikingcamping.com to read excerpts and purchase online. The website also offers updates for each book, recent reports on trails and campsites, and details about new titles such as the *Done in a Day* series.

Don't Waste Your Time in the Canadian Rockies
The Opinionated Hiking Guide

ISBN 0-9689419-7-4 Even here, in a mountain range designated a UNESCO World Heritage Site for its "superlative natural phenomena" and "exceptional natural beauty and aesthetic importance," not all scenery is equal. Some destinations are simply more striking, more intriguing, more inspiring than others. Now you can be certain you're choosing a rewarding hike for your weekend or vacation. This uniquely helpful, visually captivating guidebook covers Banff, Jasper, Kootenay, Yoho and Waterton Lakes national parks, plus Mt. Robson and Mt. Assiniboine provincial parks. It rates each trail *Premier, Outstanding, Worthwhile,* or *Don't Do,* explains why, and provides comprehensive route descriptions. 138 dayhikes and backpack trips. Trail maps for each hike. 544 pages, 270 photos, full colour throughout. 5th edition updated July 2006.

Where Locals Hike
in the Canadian Rockies
The Premier Trails in Kananaskis
Country, near Canmore and Calgary

ISBN 978-0-9783427-4-6 The 55 most rewarding dayhikes and backpack trips within two hours of Calgary's international airport. All lead to astonishing alpine meadows, ridges and peaks. Though these trails are little known compared to those in the nearby Canadian Rocky Mountain national parks, the scenery is equally magnificent. Includes Peter Lougheed and Spray Valley provincial parks. Discerning trail reviews help you choose your trip. Detailed route descriptions keep you on the path. 320 pages, 180 photos, trail maps for each hike, full colour throughout. Updated 3rd edition August 2008.

Where Locals Hike
in the West Kootenay
The Premier Trails in Southeast B.C.
near Kaslo & Nelson

ISBN 978-0-9689419-9-7 See the peaks, glaciers and cascades that make locals passionate about these mountains. The 50 most rewarding dayhikes and backpack trips in the Selkirk and west Purcell ranges of southeast British Columbia. Includes Valhalla, Kokanee Glacier, and Goat Range parks, as well as hikes near Arrow, Slocan, and Kootenay lakes. Discerning trail reviews help you choose your trip. Detailed route descriptions keep you on the path. 272 pages, 130 photos, trail locator maps, full colour throughout. Updated 2nd edition April 2007.

Camp Free in B.C.

ISBN 978-0-9735099-3-9 Make your weekend or vacation adventurous and revitalizing. Enjoy British Columbia's scenic byways and 2WD backroads—in your low-clearance car or your big RV. Follow precise directions to 350 campgrounds, from the B.C. Coast to the Rocky Mountains. Choose from 80 low-fee campgrounds similar in quality to provincial parks but half the price. Find retreats where the world is yours alone. Simplify life: slow down, ease up. Fully appreciate B.C.'s magnificent backcountry, including the Sunshine Coast, Okanagan, Shuswap Highlands, Selkirk and Purcell ranges, Cariboo Mountains, and Chilcotin Plateau. 544 pages, 200 photos, 20 regional maps, full colour throughout. Updated 4th edition April 2007.

Gotta Camp Alberta

ISBN 978-0-9735099-0-8 Make your weekend or vacation adventurous and revitalizing. Enjoy Alberta's scenic byways and 2WD backroads—in your low-clearance car or your big RV. Follow precise directions to 150 idyllic campgrounds, from the foothill lakes to the Rocky Mountains. Camp in national parks, provincial parks, and recreation areas. Find retreats where the world is yours alone. Simplify life: slow down, ease up. Return home soothed by the serenity of nature. Approximately 400 pages, 170 photos, and 18 maps. Full colour throughout. First edition June 2008.

Hiking from Here to WOW: North Cascades
50 Trails to the Wonder of Wilderness

ISBN 978-0-89997-444-6 The authors hiked more than 1,400 miles through North Cascades National Park plus the surrounding wilderness areas, including Glacier Peak, Mt. Baker, and the Pasayten. They took more than 1,000 photos and hundreds of pages of field notes. Then they culled their list of favourite hikes down to 50 trips—each selected for its power to incite awe. Their 272-page book describes where to find the cathedral forests, psychedelic meadows, spiky summits, and colossal glaciers that distinguish the American Alps. And it does so in refreshing style: honest, literate, entertaining, inspiring. Like all *WOW Guides*, this one is full colour throughout, with 180 photos and a trail map for each dayhike and backpack trip. First edition May 2007.

Hiking from Here to WOW: Utah Canyon Country
95 Trails to the Wonder of Wilderness

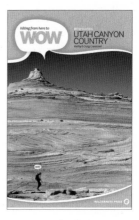

ISBN 978-0-89997-452-1 The authors hiked more than 1,600 miles through Zion, Bryce, Escalante-Grand Staircase, Glen Canyon, Grand Gulch, Cedar Mesa, Canyonlands, Moab, Arches, Capitol Reef, and the San Rafael Swell. They took more than 2,500 photos and hundreds of pages of field notes. Then they culled their list of favourite hikes down to 95 trips—each selected for its power to incite awe. Their 480-page book describes where to find the redrock cliffs, slickrock domes, soaring arches, and ancient ruins that make southern Utah unique in all the world. And it does so in refreshing style: honest, literate, entertaining, inspiring. Like all *WOW Guides*, this one is full colour throughout, with 220 photos and a trail map for each dayhike and backpack trip. First edition May 2008.

Done in a Day: Jasper
The 10 Premier Hikes

ISBN 978-0-9783427-1-5 Where to invest your limited hiking time to enjoy the greatest scenic reward. Choose an easy, vigourous, or challenging hike. Start your adventure within a short drive of town. Witness the wonder of Jasper National Park and be back for a hot shower, great meal, and soft bed. 128 pages, 75 photos, trail maps for each trip, full colour throughout. First edition December 2007.

Done in a Day: Banff
The 10 Premier Hikes

ISBN 978-0-9783427-0-8 Where to invest your limited hiking time to enjoy the greatest scenic reward. Choose an easy, vigourous, or challenging hike. Start your adventure within a short drive of town. Witness the wonder of Banff National Park and be back for a hot shower, great meal, and soft bed. 136 pages, 90 photos, trail maps for each trip, full colour throughout. First edition December 2007.

Done in a Day: Moab
The 10 Premier Hikes

ISBN 978-0-9735099-8-4 Where to invest your limited hiking time to enjoy the greatest scenic reward. Choose an easy, vigourous, or challenging hike. Start your adventure within a short drive of town. Witness the wonder of canyon country—including Arches and Canyonlands national parks—and be back for a hot shower, great meal, and soft bed. 160 pages, 110 photos, trail maps for each trip, full colour throughout. First edition February 2008.

Done in a Day: Whistler
The 10 Premier Hikes

ISBN 978-0-9735099-7-7 Where to invest your limited hiking time to enjoy the greatest scenic reward. Choose an easy, vigourous, or challenging hike. Start your adventure within a short drive of the village. Witness the wonder of Whistler, British Columbia, and be back for a hot shower, great meal, and soft bed. 144 pages, 80 photos, trail maps for each trip, full colour throughout. First edition December 2007.

Bears Beware!
How to Avoid an Encounter

The 30-minute MP3 that could save your life. Download it at hikingcamping.com (>Guidebooks >Hiking >Rockies). In bear country, ignorance = risk. Learn simple, specific strategies for safer hiking, especially how to use your voice on the trail to warn away bears. Endorsed by the wardens at Jasper and Waterton national parks.